CHINK

Chink

—

Eyes too slanted to see

Armstrong Millamena

ISBN: 1514675404
ISBN 13: 9781514675403
Library of Congress Control Number: 2015910276
CreateSpace Independent Publishing Platform
North Charleston, South Carolina

I

THE ASIAN AWAKENING

I was eating a sandwich and sipping on a latte all by myself at a Starbucks in SoHo, thinking of my various writings. I was enjoying the daylight, which was gradually turning to darkness. Abruptly, a person came up to my table and introduced himself. He said his name was Dan, or something like that. He said he recognized me from college, which was some time ago, and he knew I was a writer. I shook his hand, and he sat across from me. I didn't expect him to do that, because I didn't invite him to sit with me. Usually when someone sees another person at a table, he or she asks to sit down, or speaks while standing up until asked to sit down. Whatever the case, Dan volunteered himself to converse with me, and I recalled that I might have met him briefly in one of those various Asian clubs in college. He asked me if I was still writing. I replied yes.

He then stated, "Are you still writing about the issues?" I didn't know what he was talking about and asked him to clarify his question. He then said, "Weren't you writing about Asian issues?"

At this time, I was writing about many different things in various genres. I was also considering writing about Asian issues, because when I was in college, this was something that concerned many Asian college students.

During my college years, I did gather information from everywhere to write on Asian issues. Primarily, during college, Asian clubs would network and visit numerous universities, which had workshops and activities for Asian students. In these workshops, the students running the events would always talk about the Asian issues that affected them. I really joined these clubs to socialize, meet girls, see new things, and take advantage of the numerous activities, such as ski trips, hiking, camping, traveling to various colleges, and sleepovers. Nonetheless, the issues never really sank in with me, because the things that happened to some Asians had never happened to me. Some of the experiences occurred a long time ago, before I was born.

Yet there were some Asians who were passionate about the issues and were affected in ways I didn't understand. I do remember keeping a log of information about the Asian dilemma in my cabinet drawers, which were filled with paper notes along with other various writings. During college I considered writing about the issues and maybe completing the project sometime in the future, because the issues affected a lot of people at the time. But I stopped writing about them because they were too complex and polarizing, and I lost interest.

So when Dan approached me, I was in Starbucks, just relaxing and having some tranquil time to myself. I didn't want to be bothered nor did I have the time to go into a deep conversation and immerse myself in a sensitive topic. Thus I responded in an uncaring way, pretending I didn't know what he was saying and hoping he would cut it short. I responded, "What about the Asian issues?"

He was shocked by my comment and shook his head, asking me, "Are your eyes too slanted to see?"

I was baffled by his comment, not knowing what he was trying to get at; after all, his eyes were more slanted than mine. He said, "I can't believe you don't get it. You don't see it."

I could see he was getting a little upset. Feeling defensive, I asked, "Like what?"

He questioned me. Pulling back his chin in a slight head motion backward, surprised by my comment he said, "There's so much going on with discrimination, stereotypes, abuse, and inequality for Asians, and you ask me, 'Like what?' You and so many Asians only care about yourself. You don't see the issue and don't know what the hell is going on."

He got up and walked off. I was, without a doubt, in awe. I didn't know what to make of it. I was a bit shocked; it was a rude awakening. I viewed him as some sort of cartoon character. When I left Starbucks, I was confused and a little angry. This person interrupted me at my table while I was at peace, with my snack, and attacked me verbally without really knowing me. I admit that later that night, I couldn't sleep; I was thinking about the whole ordeal. The incident took me by surprise, and I was definitely caught off guard. I said to myself, "I should've choked that person, intruding on my personal time."

Nevertheless, as days passed, it was hard for me to continue writing, as I got writer's block with some of my subjects. I couldn't think. Then it dawned on me that maybe I should write about Asian issues. I knew I didn't want to be a writer who was considered an activist or a writer who tackles issues. However, I reminded myself that I was still a writer, and if that were the case, I should be able to write about anything. I should be just as passionate in all my writing as that individual felt about Asian issues.

So the writing began. This would be the hardest writing I ever ventured into, because I would interview and obtain feedback from literally hundreds of Asians, mainly from visiting numerous college forums. In addition, I would have to gather hard facts and evidence from many sources to back up what I was writing. This book would take many years to complete.

The main purpose of this book is to write about Asian issues as described by countless Asian individuals, groups, and so forth. It approaches the issues from numerous people's opinions and perspectives and from various angles, thus giving all Asians a voice. Furthermore, I wanted to write about Asian issues in their raw form—unedited, unrated, and true to the views of real Asians. This book is called *Chink*. As defined by *Wikipedia*, "chink" is an English ethnic slur, usually referring to a person of Chinese or East Asian ethnicity. Use of the term is often considered offensive to the Asian people.

Thus, I used *Chink* as the title so that people fully grasp and understand the significance of the word. Furthermore, I used it based on the realization of how some non-Asians perceive Asians based on this derogatory word and its definition.

As I finally finished writing about the extremely exhausting, delicate issues concerning Asian people, I chose not to provide or express in detail my own personal opinion in this book. This way, I could keep the integrity of the book true to the people I interviewed and the people I was writing the book for. In addition, I did not want to bias the book in any way by including any of my own experience or knowledge.

Therefore, people who read this book should differentiate me, as the narrator or writer, from the people I was writing the book for and the message it conveyed.

Asian issues are very sensitive, controversial, and highly complex topics to write about. It would be inappropriate for me to sugarcoat the stories or opinions relayed to me by these passionate Asian individuals. I had to present the information given to me as authentically as possible. However, this book was not intended for Asians who are weak-minded. It was not intended to create radical Asians. Asians who are criminals or have criminal minds do not represent the Asian cause; therefore, an angry Asian who goes out and does harm to anyone in the name of the Asian cause is an isolated lunatic that surely does not represent the Asian people. Moreover, Asians who have hideous personalities and vulgar attitudes and character do not represent Asians. This book was meant for the intellectual and respectful Asians who want change, respect, and awareness of Asian issues and concerns.

II

THE DILEMMA WITH ASIAN PEOPLE

The problem I ran into with the Asian people I interviewed was that they would not agree to include their names or their occupational titles for this book, because they believe Asian haters' tactics are highly sophisticated, overwhelming, and powerfully deceptive.

In this book, those discriminating against Asians are called "Asian haters." These haters are people who suppress Asians' rights and freedom and utilize every means possible to stifle Asian progress and well-being. Asian haters will also be called the "oppressors" or the "beast." The oppressors and beast have only one purpose: to destroy Asians in their entirety. Asian haters, oppressors, and the beast will be discussed in more detail shortly.

Most Asians I interviewed gave numerous reasons as to why they didn't want their names printed as a source of reference. One reason was that they didn't want to be misquoted, because sometimes when words are written in print, people interpret them differently and incorrectly. Moreover, they didn't want what they said to haunt them in the future and somehow hinder their career goals. The biggest reason why Asians didn't want to use their names and job titles in this book was because the beast and oppressors are powerful enough to manipulate facts and control media to their advantage. The oppressors own the media, including the Internet, news, and print publications. They control people and so much more. If an Asian person were to tell the truth about the issues, the beast would utilize every resource to dispute his or her claim. First, the beast would rephrase what was said, so the whole world would misinterpret the message for its own purpose.

There are tactics the Asian haters use. They are carefully orchestrated and brilliant. For example, if an Asian activist for Asian rights were interviewed, the interviewer who worked for the oppressor would not allow the Asian activist to complete an entire story and convey an honest message. The interviewer would constantly interrupt every time the Asian activist tried to make a truthful point. This technique used by the beast is an adroit maneuver to block the truth from the world. Another method used is when the oppressors try to go deep into the Asian activist's past and personal life, hoping to find any character flaw to highlight. By digging deep to find any flaw in the Asian activist's history, the oppressor's hope is for others to discount the individual and perceive the Asian activist as a liar, even if it has nothing to do with the truth being presented. These were some of the reasons why Asians I interviewed would not give me permission to use their names in this book. However, they provided me with articles as proof to back up what they tried to convey.

It made me somewhat furious. Because I could not use the real people's names that I personally interviewed as references in this book, I knew it would make me a sacrificial lamb by bringing up the issue. Therefore, people reading this book might look at me as though I'm the activist, giving my own opinion. I did *not* want that! I decided to use the facts to give a voice to these Asians who would not come forward.

A typical problem with Asian people is that they are unlike other groups that are very vocal when it comes to the issues that concern them. Asians, for the most part, are silent. The reasons could be rooted in their centuries-old culture. Hopefully, this book can change all that. In fact, this book *will* change all that. This book will be the most comprehensive book ever written about Asian issues.

For this story, America will be a microcosm of the world. In America, when non-Asians (white, black, Hispanic, or others) treat an Asian disrespectfully, they will surely treat an Asian individual anywhere in the world just as bad, or worse.

The book will discuss Asian Americans. It will also similarly represent Asians abroad, living in places where Asians are not the majority, such as Europe. These people are considered Asians growing up in Caucasian Europe. The only difference between America and Europe is that America is a country in which the Native Americans were the original inhabitants, and it is a melting pot of people from all over the world. Countries in Europe are slightly different. To clarify, in European countries, the Caucasian people were originally from those European countries, with Asians immigrating there. However, America began with Native Americans who first roamed the land, and then people from everywhere started to immigrate to the country, beginning with the Europeans. Hence, there are more Europeans in America than any other people.

To understand the issues, I needed to understand the underlying problem. As I interviewed countless people and researched different issues, Asian individuals stated their cases, gave me their personal opinions, and provided news articles and excerpts from various mediums to back it up. I decided to present the opinions of only those Asians that could provide proof from various articles to make the case for unfairness.

In addition, to understand Asian issues, you need to understand the fundamentals of discrimination, prejudice, and all the terms that describe withholding the rights and fair chance for Asians to have equality. Having said that, Asians must accept the fact that these issues exist, and they should not shy away or run. In fact, Asians must embrace this reality and then challenge these issues with their utmost effort and strength.

III

WHO ARE THE ASIAN HATERS, THE OPPRESSORS, OR THE BEAST?

They come from all walks of human society, including Asians themselves, which will be discussed in greater detail later.

There are three categories of Asian haters:

1. The white supremacists who hate Asians
2. Nonwhites (people of color) of various ethnicities who hate Asians
3. Asians who hate Asians

LET'S START OUT BY DEFINING WHO THESE PEOPLE ARE:

The first category explained to me by Asians I interviewed consists of white supremacist groups or individuals. It's important to add that this book shouldn't be interpreted as proposing that all Caucasian people are oppressors of Asians—that logic would be flawed, prejudiced, and grossly incorrect. I would take no part in that interpretation. This book only focuses on those white supremacist groups or individuals who discriminate and do everything in their power to deny Asians their rights, liberty, and advancement.

The oppression of Asians started centuries ago, when Caucasians originating from Europe came to Asian countries to implement imperialism and enforce slavery or get cheap labor from Asia for their own purposes and benefits. In earlier times in America, white supremacists were the Ku Klux Klan (KKK) or neo-Nazi skinheads (the white power group). White supremacists nowadays have become more sophisticated and don't have to wear a white, cone-shaped hat with a white costume or shave their heads like neo-Nazi skinheads to be white supremacists. They live among us like ordinary, everyday people, and differentiating a white supremacist from an ordinary white person is extremely difficult. White supremacists are racist and extremely prejudiced, but they won't display or manifest it to the world conspicuously. Nonetheless, their actions are sometimes evident. Ronald Ebens, a white American, killed Vincent Chin, a Chinese American, because he thought Chin was Japanese. He is an example of a white person who doesn't wear the KKK's white, cone-shaped hat with a white costume or shave his head to be identified as a racist or part of a white supremacist group. He is a great example of an everyday, normal-looking individual who could assimilate with everyone but hid a true color of prejudice in his heart and soul from the public. The Vincent Chin story will be discussed in greater detail in later chapters. You could read about his story in many articles, such as the one from the *New York Times* titled "Why Vincent Chin Matters" by Frank H. Wu. Another example of white-supremacist individuals or groups who utilized their powers to discriminate against Asians or any people of color occurred during the 1800s in America. White Americans, who originally came from Europe, created the Exclusion Laws, banning Asians living in America from voting, owning property, or legally immigrating to America.

The second category of oppressors consists of nonwhites who hate Asians. These people are of various ethnicities and are from non-European regions, such as Africa; Asia; North, South, and Central America; the Middle East; and so forth. These people of color jump on the bandwagon of hating Asians based on their belief of various myths that Asians are weird, strange, mysterious, and evil. They also base their knowledge on what they learn incorrectly from the media or ignorant people.

For example, there is a well-known professional boxer who likes to denigrate Asians every chance he gets. If you search his comments on Google or Twitter, they will say it all. In one of his many comments, he said he would let Manny Pacquiao, another professional boxer, serve him sushi rolls and cook him rice. However, Manny Pacquiao is Filipino, not Japanese. In February 2012 he tweeted, "Jeremy Lin"—a professional basketball player—"is a good player, but all the hype is because he's Asian."

Many Asians believe wholeheartedly that his comments were condescending, uncalled for, and unacceptable. Asians are not necessarily saying nor could they prove that he's a racist individual, only that his remarks could be perceived that way. Nonetheless, there are many people of color, whether black, Hispanic, or from other nonwhite groups, that do carry prejudice against Asians. And as stated in the earlier passage, it shouldn't be interpreted that all people of color are prejudiced against Asian people, but this book provides examples of people of color who are prejudiced against Asian people.

The third and deadliest category contains the worst oppressors of all. They hide under Asian faces, like wolves in sheep's clothing, but devour the Asian cause with no remorse. They are Asians that are considered "Twinkies" or "coconuts." They are Asians who hate Asians.

What is a Twinkie? A Twinkie is an Asian whose color is yellow, based on the pigment of his or her skin, but whose internal thinking or state of mind is that of a white Caucasian individual. The name comes from the Hostess cake, Twinkie, which is yellow on the outside and white on the inside. Similarly, a Twinkie is someone who, from the surface, obviously looks Asian but acts like a white person, trying to emulate the way a white person thinks, talks, dresses, eats, and walks. This can be said of some Asian Americans growing up in America, trying to be white Americans, or of some Asians growing up in Europe, trying to be white Europeans and discounting their Asian heritage and characteristics to the best of their ability. Even in some Asian countries, like China, women are having eyelid surgeries to look more like white women. This is the influence of the beast, which displays in the media that the European women's eye features are acceptable, but Asians' are not. A Twinkie is a term used for an Asian with a lighter shade of yellow skin pigment, from countries such as China, Japan, Korea, Taiwan, and so forth.

What is a coconut? The meaning of the term coconut is similar to Twinkie, but these Asian people originated in warmer climates, such as the Philippines, Malaysia, Indonesia, and Thailand. The term is generally applied to Asians with darker, brown skin. The comparison is made to a coconut, which is brown on the outside and white inside. Twinkies and coconuts are Asian people who just can't be themselves and try so hard to be something else, hoping to be accepted by their white peers or mainstream society.

Twinkies and coconuts carry a false sense of security. They think that by acting like white people they will be fully accepted, and their Asian ethnicities will no longer be a factor or issue. Nonetheless, as discussed further in later chapters, that is not the case.

HOW WERE TWINKIES AND COCONUTS CREATED?

Twinkies and coconuts were created for numerous reasons. I will discuss only a few. One of the reasons is that Asians who grow up in predominately white communities have to assimilate with their white neighbors or else live lives without communication. Thus, you can't fully blame Asians for trying to fit in, because they can't grow up in a white community without working along with their white neighbors. Asian individuals, whether Asian Americans or Asians in Europe, need to find acceptance and get along with white people. Nevertheless, the Twinkies and coconuts are eager to be accepted by whites, even if it means being denigrated and humiliated by them.

TWINKIES AND COCONUTS
Twinkies and coconuts sometimes grow up in white communities and, as children, are made fun of and ridiculed because of their Asian descent. They then do their best to disassociate from their own culture and ethnicities just to be accepted by whites. When these Asians grow up, they frown at Asian people; they are unable to forget the persecution they received as children growing up in a predominately white neighborhood.

Therefore, these particular Asians, if they are not strong enough mentally to fight the power, break down and become Twinkies or coconuts. They start looking down at Asians and rarely associating with them. They want to hang out, communicate, and associate mostly with non-Asian people. Moreover, these Twinkies and coconuts are brainwashed, wired, and transformed to believe they are better than their Asian counterparts. This is because they grew up with whites, and they disregard their Asian culture and origin. Furthermore, some of these Asians from a white upbringing pathetically believe they are now truly white people. On the same note, some Asians who grow up in predominately black or Hispanic communities are in the same predicament and want to be black or Hispanic.

The best analogy to explain what transforms an Asian into a Twinkie or coconut is to compare the situation to aliens coming to Earth from Mars. The aliens are Martians, and they are the oppressors. And the innocent Asians from Earth are the human beings being oppressed.

One day the Martians land on Earth and greet the Asian human beings as friends. Afterward, some Asians look at these Martians as friendly neighbors. However, the Martians have their own objective and plan to someday conquer the entire Asian race and make Asians the ultimate slaves, mentally and physically. The aliens are brilliant in how they accomplish their goals and mission by marketing their Martian society to the world. They begin to create numerous Martian products, such as medicine, beverages, food, clothes, appliances, and other things. They make movies and music displaying Martian entertainment and broadcast them nationally. They design clothes and fashion and show them to the world. The aliens ingeniously provide an endless amount of products and services that cater to Asian needs.

As time passes, Asians begin to buy what the aliens sell, watching and listening to the everyday life of Martians through the media and using the various products and services offered by the Martians. Thus, Asians become so overwhelmed and inundated by the monopoly and dominance of the Martians that some Asians themselves want to become Martians. Asians gradually become helpless from the incredible mind game played by the Martians, and some Asians become brainwashed and forget themselves along the way. The masterful technique, designed craftily by the aliens, transforms Asians to become Martians. The Martians have Asians do anything they can to join and protect the aliens from Mars at the Asians' expense.

This is the best way of explaining what creates a Twinkie or coconut. The non-Asian oppressors manipulate and psychologically twist the minds of some Asians so that they no longer want to be Asians.

Twinkies and coconuts in turn become the worst oppressors of Asian people. They look down at Asians; they rarely want to socialize with Asians. If Twinkies and coconuts have positions of power, they do not hire Asians and prefer to marry non-Asians. You see some of these Twinkies and coconuts as news broadcasters or actors in movies and in the entertainment field. They pretend to represent Asians, but they are really using that facade to move up the ladder of success for their own benefit, not the benefit of Asians. Twinkies and coconuts are real fakes.

Another reason why Twinkies and coconuts exist is simply because some Asians don't want to be Asians and want to be part of another race. Some African Americans commented that what I was writing was similar to what they see in their own communities as "Oreo cookies"—African Americans who want to be white. They compare these individuals with Oreos: black on the outside and white on the inside. Africans Americans do not consider this "cool" or "hip."

Twinkies and coconuts are the most dangerous people for Asians. They would exterminate the entire Asian race if they could, just to find acceptance by their Caucasian counterparts. An example is World War II, when Imperial Japan wanted to follow Hitler's white-power Germany as an ally and conquer and annihilate its Asian neighbors. In fact, some Japanese at the time craftily shaved their moustaches in a way that emulated Hitler's moustache, and they followed his ruthless killing ways—just like Twinkies, in a way.

Nonetheless, the post–World War II thinking was immensely negative toward the Japan of the past, and Japan paid a heavy price for it, as many Asian countries showed tremendous animosity against Japan for its wrongdoing. Hopefully, Japan and new, emerging Asian countries learn from history and do not follow the same path as Japan did in World War II, disrespecting their Asian neighbors. In modern-day society, hopefully Twinkies and coconuts will also educate themselves about the past and abandon their brainwashed, cult-thinking way.

How do you know if you are a Twinkie or coconut or transforming into one?

If you are using more than 50 percent of your time to do non-Asian activities, then you are a Twinkie or coconut or could possibly morph into one. Most non-Asians don't consume anywhere close to 50 percent of their time by watching, listening, or participating in Asian activities or lifestyles, so why should Asians spend their valuable time and money on non-Asian society?

Nonetheless, there are a few elite Asians who are considered the cream of the crop, the best of the best. These selected Asians see the conniving scheme of the oppressors and don't fall for their tricks. The elite, intelligent, and independent Asians will prosper from knowledge; however, they must also make it their goal to educate those lost Asians (Twinkies and coconuts) and stop the cancer from spreading globally.

IV

THE COMPARISON OF ASIAN AMERICANS AND ASIANS LIVING IN ASIA

Let's examine the advantages and disadvantages of Asian Americans compared to Asians living in Asia.

One advantage Asian Americans have is that they understand people from all over the world hands down, because America is a melting pot of various countries, ethnicities, religions, and cultures. Asians abroad have to realize that there are many different types of Americans in America. The original Americans were the American Indians, who first roamed the land before the name America was ever established in the country. Thereafter, Europeans immigrated to the land, made it their home, and are now considered white Americans. European immigrants are the majority of the population in America, and they control the country and make its policies. Asians who immigrated to America and made it their home are now considered Asian Americans. Africans who immigrated to the land and made it their home are considered African Americans. Natives of South and Central America who immigrated to the land and made it their home are now considered Hispanic Americans, and the list goes on. Therefore, Asian Americans interact directly with various nationalities on an everyday basis.

Asian Americans know white Americans, as well as Americans of color, from early childhood. Asian Americans are able to fully observe prejudices of white Americans and nonwhite Americans from early childhood into adulthood. Thus, Asian Americans experience prejudice throughout their lifetimes and see individuals or groups of people, whether white Americans or nonwhites, and know that prejudice exists hidden among their hearts. They are very knowledgeable about racist people and can see through the fake façades that hide hatred. Asian Americans can see how a prejudiced non-Asian child transitions to an adult, who could pretend not to be prejudiced but holds a personal, hidden bias from past history that's within—a prejudice that cannot be hidden by a fake smile or dressed formally to create the perception of a decent individual.

In comparison, Asians living in Asia may not be as knowledgeable about racism as Asian Americans, because they may not grow up or have real contact with various nationalities. Asians abroad, growing up with their own Asian people, may only observe white or nonwhite Americans through movies, TV, music, and radio. However, in these mediums, Americans are usually superheroes—the righteous, the romantics, the good, and the white knights in shining armor ready to save the day. These mediums do not project that some Americans are racist beyond one's wildest imagination and would enslave Asians for their benefit. Therefore, when Asians come to America or a European country for the first time, they may experience a rude awakening of bias. A good example would be an ignorant Asian traveling to Nazi Germany in World War II, thinking Germans are great, and then ending up in a concentration camp, ready to be exterminated. Knowledge is power, and Asian Americans know a little bit more about whites and nonwhites from various countries because they grow up with them, as opposed to some Asians living abroad who don't.

Asian Americans also face disadvantages. Because prejudice exists against Asian Americans, they are unable to excel in certain fields, like sports. The reason lies not in their performances, but in the uncontrollable factor of non-Asian coaches not taking them seriously. For instance, an Asian person could be the best athlete in the world, but if the coach or assistants don't allow the individual to play, then the athlete is invisible. Take, for example, Jeremy Lin, who used to play for the New York Knicks in the NBA; once the Knicks allowed him more playing time, he was able to showcase his true talents, but this happened only because some players on his team were injured. If those players were not on the injured list, Jeremy Lin would not have been given playing time, because stereotypes in America make people believe that Asians can't compete in sports.

In addition, during childhood, Asian Americans are overlooked and ignored by non-Asian coaches, athletic directors, and faculties. This discourages young, talented Asians in America from pursuing sports. Moreover, due to Asian culture's style of bringing up children in America, Asian parents don't approve of their children focusing primarily on sports instead of academics.

On the other hand, Asians who grow up in Asia have advantages, such as self-empowerment. Based on the simple fact that Asians living in Asia are not held back by the same uncontrollable factors, such as a non-Asian society discouraging them from playing sports, overlooking them, or holding them back, Asians abroad are able to fine-tune their athletic capabilities and excel in their sports. For example, most well-known Asian athletes in America are imports from Asia, not Asian Americans, such as Hideki Matsui or "Godzilla," a former New York Yankee from Japan; Yao Ming, a former NBA player from China; Manny Pacquiao, a professional world-champion boxer from the Philippines; and many others. The talented athletes living in Asia are not held back by prejudiced non-Asian society writing them off. That is why in the Olympics, there are many talented Asian athletes from abroad winning an incredible number of Olympic medals, as opposed to Asian American athletes.

Now we understand whom the Asian haters, oppressors, or the beast are and have distinguished the advantages and disadvantages of Asians growing up in America versus Asians growing up in Asia. The following chapter will discuss the numerous problems resulting in Asians ending up as innocent victims, discriminated against and felled at the mercy of the beast. The problems of Asians are vast and need to be addressed and corrected only by Asians.

V

WHY ASIANS IN AMERICA AND ASIANS OVERSEAS ACQUIRED THESE PROBLEMS IN THE FIRST PLACE

The following information discusses the problems that will hold Asians back from liberty, respect, and the pursuit of happiness, unless Asians change and do something about them. The issues and concerns are not based on fictional stories but on absolute facts.

Problem 1: Asians Allow Non-Asians to Portray Asians in Disparaging Ways and Don't Challenge the Media
The reason people think of Asians in derogatory ways is because Asians allow non-Asians to portray them in that fashion. The non-Asian media outlets always show Asians in a bad light. It has already been established through the white media that only Asians can change this by challenging it. However, since the beginning of time, the media has made Asians ashamed of themselves. Mainstream society has made Asians look like weirdos through movies, television, and writings.

Some Asian Americans as well as Asians overseas have started believing this. As a result, their self-esteem starts to deteriorate, and they let their true potential wither away.

The oppressors are continuously looking for new and creative ways to fool Asians without them knowing it. The oppressors plan it that way so that they have the advantage. Asians should always vehemently challenge wrongful portrayals by non-Asians. The psychological torture used by the media is very similar to that of a war when it comes to denigrating and disrespecting people.

In mainstream movies and television, white Americans or Europeans, and some people of color, have emotions; they laugh, cry, play, and have personalities. Asians, on the other hand, are perceived to be inhuman—Asian men are evil, and Asian women are promiscuous. The non-Asian-controlled media contrived it that way. It makes it easier for ignorant people to hate Asian men and downgrade Asian women. It also makes it easier for non-Asians to discriminate against Asians as a whole without feeling that they're doing anything wrong.

The media has done an incredible and convincing job of making the Asian male look like a stupid, geeky, nonsexual imbecile. Why didn't the male Asian population do anything about these stereotypes that give them a deplorable status and only make them seem more foolish? The oppressors, with their grand scheme of propaganda, have done an extraordinary job for which they are now clapping their hands. They demoralized Asians through various mediums as they positioned Asians just where they wanted them to be...viewed as idiots. Asians are depicted so badly in the media that many Asians are convinced by it and hating themselves as well. It's another grand old plan to have all Asians hate and fight each other.

Problem 2: Asian Women Are Portrayed as Promiscuous Sex Objects, and Asian Women Don't Fight Against It

Asian women were given a bigger advantage than Asian men, because the beast exposed them as exotic, sexual, and sensual beings. Asian women are viewed by the media as pretty, promiscuous, sexual animals, and some Asian women actually use that asset to advance in society. Asian women, in the eyes of the beast, are not looked at as a threat, unlike Asian men. That is why you see many more Asian women on mainstream TV broadcasts, movies, and the corporate ladder; white America feels it can always put the Asian women in check and in their places, which they cannot do with Asian males. Asian women are put on pedestals because of sex, and some Asian women love the attention. What woman doesn't want to be thought of as sexy, exotic, and beautiful? However, there is looming danger in the future for Asian women if they're only thought of as sex objects.

To illustrate the point further, the media usually portrays Asian women in the movies as sex objects and promiscuous. I know that Asian women don't want that image. I'm sure that all Asian women want to be respected, and they don't want to be portrayed as easy, submissive individuals. Asian women would like others to think of them as intelligent people who deserve to be taken seriously.

In order for this to change, Asian women have to demand respect from those who are creating this misperception. Even though some Asian women love the fact that they are viewed as desirable, exotic, and beautiful, there will always be a backlash. And sometimes the backlash can be deadly.

For example, when Asian women walk the streets, sometimes ignorant non-Asian men may approach them and think they're easy, because they are supposed to be submissive, based on movies and other media. If these women are reluctant to give in to these ignorant men's demands, they may get hurt or raped.

When Asian women enter the corporate world, they may not be taken seriously, because they may be looked at only as sex toys. Furthermore, if Asian women do climb the corporate ladder to become supervisors, managers, or executives, their subordinates may not take them seriously. They may think of Asian women as sex objects, not individuals who should have power. Thus, there is a tremendous backlash and disadvantage if Asian women don't change people's perceptions of them.

How to change these perceptions is up to Asian women. For those Asian women who do love the sexual attention, this may have some negative long-term effects in their personal lives as they mature. Asian females should be aware of the trickle-down effect of being considered easy and cheap. It's up to them to speak out and fight to get that respect.

Problem 3: Asians Don't Realize How Prejudice Is Used against Them in the Privacy of Non-Asian Homes and Through the Media, to the Advantage of the Oppressors
The oppressors use prejudice as a gargantuan tool for crushing economic success of competitors such as Asians. The beast creates market perception and convinces the world not to buy what Asians wear or not to watch Asian movies. Prejudice can be taught in many forms, directly or indirectly; either form can be equally powerful.

Asian hatred is taught both ways by oppressors. It's also no surprise that the media reaffirms those negative portrayals about Asians through movies and TV. If you take the time to analyze and research within the last century, you will realize that countless old movies such as *The Octagon*, starring Chuck Norris; *Bloodsport*, with Jean-Claude Van Damme; *The Karate Kid, Part II*, with Ralph Macchio; and many, many more, have main themes of an Asian master training a white person to beat up Asian people. In oppressors' eyes, Asians are supposed to be evil people, and other nationalities are good people. The movies show an Asian teaching a non-Asian to go against an Asian; thus, they hate Asians. It's an absolute brilliant idea to brainwash the world against Asians. Bravo!

One person I interviewed said, "You rarely see movies where a Caucasian trainer teaches an Asian person wrestling or boxing, only to have [that Asian person] beat up white people and end up with the white girl."

Many other moviemakers love portraying Asians as creepy people or nerds. Asians should review films from the past created by non-Asians, that include Asians, and the films will say it all. This is what the beast wants the world to think Asians are—hideous and evil...the grand plan at its best.

Asians Don't Fully Understand the Negative Tactics Used by the Oppressors

Some Asians cannot see how the oppressors figure out and ultimately use certain tactics to their advantage. The challenge is for Asians to finally acknowledge this.

There are some direct tactics used against Asians:

1) Some non-Asians have negative discussions about Asians at home during dinner at the kitchen table.
2) Some non-Asians make fun of Asians in school or at the workplace and other environments.

There are also indirect tactics used against Asians:

1) The oppressors make movies showing that Asians are nerds and geeks.
2) The oppressors make movies showing that Asians are wimps.
3) The oppressors make movies showing that Asians are evil.
4) The oppressors usually don't show many Asians with normal personalities in movies.

Manipulating the mind is also an economic take-over; it's big business in the grand scheme of things. The best example would be if the beast could brainwash all Asians and control their minds, causing them to buy all of the beast's products and services. This would bankrupt any Asian businesses trying to compete with the beast.

Therefore, the oppressors must use a particular equation formulated for Asians so that the oppressors become filthy rich and powerful at the expense of Asians. At a certain point, the final outcome would be that Asians become the bitches of the oppressors…just the way the beast planned it!

For example, imagine an Asian owns a gigantic mall. This humongous mall sells every conceivable Asian product and service, such as medicine, stationery, food, cars, TV, radio, and numerous electronic devices. It also provides medical treatment and so forth. Not too far from the Asian mall is another competing mall, but this mall has non-Asian-created products and services that equal the products and services that the Asian mall provides.

In a fair competition with the rival malls, one mall would prosper over the other only if the products and services were considered better as far as quality, performance, customer satisfaction, and so forth. Nevertheless, if the Asian mall is doing better, based on superior products and services, the other mall may use a different strategy to compete. It will use prejudice, polarization, and discrimination as tools, hoping to brainwash the public through propaganda in the media to get the greater market share for its business. Therefore, the mall is using unfair tactics for its benefit.

Another great example is when Toyota cars, which originated in Japan, were considered unsafe because of faulty brakes. This occurred at the end of 2009 and the start of 2010. Given the fact that Japanese cars were out-selling American cars, the American lawmakers had a field day. Congress and the media showed fault with the Japanese cars, hoping Toyota would lose its market share and that this would help US carmakers to rebound and prosper. During that time, some Japanese people stated to me that the public seemed so against Japanese cars. It is interesting that American carmakers had many recalls on their vehicles for being unsafe, but these recalls didn't carry the same negative tone or rhetoric.

It must be Asian parents and educators that teach Asian children, so when they grow up, they know how the world works against Asians. And it's up to the Asian elite to educate all Asians, worldwide, about Asian issues.

Problem 4: Asians Are Unaware of the Formula Oppressors Use Against Them

Asians don't see or understand the mathematical equation of how oppressors work:

- Oppressors want to brainwash Asians regarding what to buy, wear, watch, and eat.
- Oppressors want to control the wages Asians get paid (keeping wages at a minimum) similar to when Asians were indentured servants in the past.
- Oppressors want to limit the powers Asians possess and do not want to give them any political power.
- Oppressors want Asians to become Twinkies and co-conuts, so that Asians can go against Asians.

Problems 5: Some Asians Are Too Naive to Understand the Polarization Technique Used by the Oppressors

The beast uses polarization as a tool to denigrate Asians and uses it to its advantage. And some Asians are too stupid to know it. The beast's business plan is to monopolize all Asian businesses; unfairness works to the advantage of the beast. The beast already polarizes Asians by not including Asians, involving Asians, or buying what Asians have to sell. Asians have to understand that they are being polarized and constrained by the oppressors. If Asians don't understand that and utilize the same tactics and techniques that are imposed on them by the oppressors, then the oppressors will enslave and profit from Asians forever. The beast polarizes Asians and doesn't value Asians as existing individuals with lives that count in modern society. With this technique used against them, Asians won't advance.

Problem 6: Asians Are Gullible to the Tactics Oppressors Use to Create Disunity among Asians

Asians become part of the problem when oppressors want to consider all Asians alike. Oppressors don't want to differentiate among Asians, because it helps their cause for prejudice and causes Asians to fight with each other. For example, oppressors like to poke fun and joke about a Chinese person, calling him or her Japanese, or make fun of a Korean person by saying that person is Vietnamese or vice versa. Oppressors like to joke that all Asians look alike. By doing this, Asian individuals have to clarify, stating they are of a particular nationality from the Pacific, not the one that the beast purposely and derogatively guesses. This causes Asian individuals to hate another Asian race.

Asians overlook the true intention of the beast, which is trying to cut off networking among various nationalities within the Asian community. This is a form of breaking the communication of Asians and keeping them separated as opposed to united. It's a warlike tactic to dismantle unity among Asians, divide them, and conquer them. There are no rules or regulations when the beast wants to take over. Asians miss the fact that the beast gets each Asian nation to go against another, which is instrumental for self-destruction. By stereotyping all Asians as the beast sees them, with the rest of the "chinks," and only recognizing bad traits and ways, some white oppressors are ingeniously using that tactical warfare to destroy Asian unity. Nonetheless, Asians never use the same tactics on those particular white oppressors, stating all whites look alike and poking fun at white people, trying to figure out if they are Irish, English, Australian, German, or some other white race.

Problem 7: Asians Don't See the Psychological Game the Oppressors Play

Asians don't heed the fact that the oppressors constantly think of ways to kill an Asian. The oppressors do it psychologically, evasively, and secretly, devising a plan to eliminate Asians by way of engraining absolute mental slavery. The psychological brainwash of the media means the more you show other nationalities (not Asians) on TV and the big screen, as well as on other mediums, the more people like and love those non-Asian individuals that are showcased. Similarly, the less you show Asians in the media, the less likely the audience is to care about them.

Problem 8: Asians Who Don't Get Involved in Asian Issues and Just Trust Society Are in a Cult

A major problem is that some Asians who do not want to get involved in Asian issues are blind and are very much in a cult. They believe in just trusting society and accepting what the oppressors do to them. It is very similar to Jonestown, which happened in the 1960s. A pastor named Jim Jones promised a society free of economic and racial divides. Jones sold a vision of peaceful harmony. When he recruited temple members, they bought into it, and he led them to the edge of destruction and used their trust to give them a final push. In the end, Jones convinced his followers to drink poison that would kill them. This is similar to the plight of the uninvolved Asians; they believe they are living in a society free of economic and racial divides, in peaceful harmony with everyone. The beast one day takes their trust, poisoning the belief of tranquility. The oppressors ultimately kill them by killing their dreams, freedom, careers, equality, and so much more.

So many Asians, who mind their own business and think Asians are treated fairly, will someday realize they joined a cult that recruited them by media without them even knowing it. Those Asians who are uninvolved with Asian issues and plan to mind their own business and do nothing about the concerns of Asians are the ones that will drown and be poisoned to death by ignorance. They will not create change to better Asians. Therefore, it is up to the passionate, driven Asians who want change to save fellow Asians. So Asians must think of which side they want to join. Do they want change, or do they want to continue living with disrespect in their everyday lives?

Problem 9: Asians Allow the Oppressors to Dictate Their Lives and Control Their Minds

Unfortunately, Asians continue to let the oppressors dictate their lives with rules, using media means to overwhelm the decisions of the majority of Asians. For example, the beast tells Asians, through the media, what's in fashion, what to wear, what movies to watch, what music to listen to, and so forth, because the beast controls what is broadcast to the public. Asians buy into it and use their valuable time and money. Asians are being force-fed by the media, which is brainwashing their minds. The media has a way to control your thoughts and ideas, and, if weak, you will submit.

It is the beast's game plan to control Asians minds through these various controlled medium they own. Oppressors do things to try to make you think the way they want you to think, and when you accept their rationale, you're beat. Once brainwashed, you accept abuse against yourself and begin to think it's OK. It's truly not OK! You are like a rape victim, thinking it is your fault. Every time an Asian accepts a medium, such as television, movies, music, magazines, or literature, without an Asian involved in it, it is like taking a pill that controls you until you become a zombie. Then you join a cult of no return. Asians should not let the oppressors spread their subliminal messages through these mediums that tries to control the Asian mind. The beast loves seeing Asians thinking like slaves, their minds held captive, without freethinking. Asians willingly allow the oppressors to control most of their businesses, and they become chained by the oppressors' rules. Asians have to break free and come back to their senses and once again take control of their minds before there is a complete genocide of the Asian mind.

Problem 10: Asians Are Easily Fooled by Fake Diplomacy of the Oppressors

Asians don't realize that fake diplomacy by the beast is utilized in the beginning stages. They use a good first impression to win the hearts and minds of Asians. The beast first approaches Asians in a nonthreatening way. Then, once they win Asians' trust, they conquer and take over, and Asians lose everything. Burglars and criminals use the same strategy; they pretend to help, and they present themselves as friends. But as time goes by, they get comfortable with you, and when you least expect it, they rob and kill you. At a moment's notice, the beast will betray Asians, and Asians will be at the beast's mercy, lose absolutely everything, and eventually become slaves.

The mistake Asians made in the past was thinking about their non-Asian neighbors as peaceful and friendly, while their non-Asian neighbors thought about take-over, dominance, and the ultimate takedown. It was an unfair thought process that Asians overlooked, and they paid the price for it. Hawaii is a great example of an Asian country that was taken over. When the oppressors went to Hawaii, they presented themselves as friends. But as time passed, they planned to conquer the people and the land, and Hawaii was *annexed* by the oppressors. Asians should learn from this and never again be fooled by *fake diplomacy*. Asians should never lower their guards and should take precaution when dealing with non-Asian oppressors.

Problem 11: Some Asians Sell Out

Some Asians let economics affect their decision-making. This essentially means that sometimes Asians are doing great in their personal businesses and make money with the oppressors, so they do not care about the Asian cause as a whole and sell out. Thus, the beast uses them as an instrument to crush the Asian cause, and they side with it for economic reasons. They are then similar to Twinkies, coconuts, or traitors.

Problem 12: Some Asians Are Too Ignorant to Understand What's Going On around Them

Unfortunately, some Asians are too dumb to realize that they also give the three categories of oppressors celebrity status. Asians worship these oppressors through television, music, movies, and so forth; thus, Asians who follow these things become destroyed personally and mentally and eventually transform into Twinkies or coconuts.

Asians cannot improve if they worship the unrighteous and place the oppressors (actors, actresses, athletes, and famous celebrities) on pedestals. Asians must create their own icons within the Asian community.

In the *Narrative of the Life of Frederick Douglass*, Frederick Douglass, an American slave, states, "It is the wish of most masters within my knowledge to keep their slaves ignorant."

In some respect, the oppressors are the Asian masters, and Asians are kept ignorant for the purpose of the oppressors' objectives. Asians need to educate themselves about what's going on around them.

Problem 13: Asians Choose to Be Foolish and Dumb about Their Past

Asians don't understand and evaluate history to the fullest, because they either foolishly don't want to, or they ignore it. It's imperative that Asians know how the oppressors operate and how they can take all their property, along with their souls, and still brilliantly portray Asians as the bad guys. The beast should not manipulate Asians like children, getting Asians to do whatever they please. All Asians must educate themselves about the past and know how they were fooled and conquered. Asians shouldn't allow the oppressors to control them. Many Asians don't think like leaders but would rather be followers or peasants, waiting for a handout. Asians must change that thought process.

Problem 14: Asians are unaware of how the oppressors were raised, how they were taught, and how they think.

Asians just don't get it about some non-Asians. Some non-Asian oppressors are educated differently from ordinary, loving human beings. They are taught incorrectly about Asians, in the living rooms of their homes. They see only derogatory things about Asians through various mediums, such as television, news, or movies. Some white oppressors who are brought up with a white-supremacist attitude are not able to see the point of view of Asians, because they are fixated in their upbringing from a white-power perspective.

Some whites think of themselves as a privileged group of people who should get everything they want and that all people of color are slaves and should serve and follow them. Given their upbringing and the white-supremacist culture, trying to change their persona and behavior is futile. Nonetheless, they need to be challenged.

The mind-sets of Asians have to change. Most Asians acquired the culture of modesty, humbleness, and passivity. Asians learned to respect everyone and kept among themselves as peaceful people. Nevertheless, some non-Asian people see that as a weakness of Asians and have a different mentality. Some non-Asians trained their people to think differently and conquered Asian people aggressively and ruthlessly, doing whatever it takes to have full control of Asians. It is critical for Asians to know this to survive and protect their livelihood. In addition, Asians must also realize that not all non-Asians are educated the same way as peace-loving Asians. Some have common sense, and others don't, depending on how they were raised or educated.

Problem 15: Asians Must Realize That Most Non-Asians Get Their Education about Asians from the Media
Uneducated non-Asians usually get their education about Asians from the media, which is inaccurate most of the time, not from a formal educational institution. Therefore, non-Asians get the wrong knowledge about Asians, directed and orchestrated by the oppressors. Therefore, Asians must make

it mandatory for educational institutions to teach Asian studies so that students get the correct education about Asians.

Problem 16: Some Asians Give Other Asians a Bad Image
Of course, there are those Asians who are extremely repulsive
and make you shy away from being Asian. There are Asians
who dress weird, don't comb their hair, eat funny, and walk
and talk like they're the most uneducated and stupid people
on earth. It has nothing to do with their lifestyle. It's pure
ignorance, similar to that of a two-year-old child leaving spa-
ghetti stains around his or her mouth after eating, or wearing
a superhero costume every day. This is not the normal behavior of a mature adult. These Asians are actually oblivious
to their actions, because they didn't take the time to educate
themselves about how non-Asians perceive their everyday
behavior. Sadly, due to circumstance, some of these Asians
are cast out by non-Asian society, and they become hermits,
sheltered in their own world. It is like they were living under
a rock for a very, very long time, not knowing what's going
on with the outside world and not understanding that what
they do is judged and critiqued. These Asians are joked about
and made spectacles of, and the Asian haters love to showcase
these particular individuals to the world for their objectives.

Unfortunately, some Asian Americans or recent Asian
immigrants do not have any social skills, because they are
too busy studying and working hard. Selfishly, they are only
thinking about themselves; they do not have time to interact
with numerous diverse, everyday people of various nationalities or to learn how to communicate with them. Therefore,

these isolated, ignorant Asians develop unappealing and re-pulsive personalities. It only helps the oppressors make fun of Asians even more. Some Asians need to work on their per-sonalities and people skills. They must understand society as a whole, how it works, and how it affects them.

Problem 17: Many Asian Men Don't Care about Their Physical Aspects and Well-Being

The reason why many Asian females betrayed Asian males by marrying white men is because some Asian males have be-trayed themselves. They didn't see the whole picture. Some Asian men didn't care about their physical appearance or personality. Asian men weren't able to figure out the balance between being studious, and exercising and being sociable. Hence, many Asians' statures are looked at and perceived as scrawny, weak, and frail. Asians must change that. Asians must take into account factors that may make them unappealing, reinvent themselves, and consider other alternatives to make themselves more attractive and appealing. Therefore, Asians must work their bodies to perfection and improve their social skills. Moreover, all Asians must try to look good, be smart, and have a likable, pleasing personality.

Problem 18: Asians Don't Fight for Credit They Deserve

Asians don't do enough to fight for the credit that they de-serve for helping America and the world prosper. When some non-Asian countries see China developing the nuclear bomb, going to space, and innovating their high-tech systems, they accuse the Chinese of stealing that technology. Presumptively, the Chinese (or Asians), in their opinion, are too stupid to be that innovative. They don't consider the history of Asians, including when Marco Polo visited and stole many Asian ideas. If they were to do their research, they would know the vast number of innovations that Asia has provided to the world. The beast or oppressors try their best to get sole, unjustifiable credit for themselves. The oppressors have others' help in creating something great but only have their faces shown to the world and hide their teammates. Similarly, Asians built railroads in America, but the history books never really show Asian faces, instead highlighting European railroad workers. There are many more examples of Asians contributing to America and the world without getting credit for it. Asians must do a better job showing their contributions to the world. When writers for the oppressors are able to make their own history, it enables them to have more power, and it somewhat justifies not sharing that recognition with anyone else.

Problem 19: Asians Need to Meticulously Evaluate Themselves and Ask the Question, "What Will It Take to Change the World's Perception about Asians?"

How stupid is an Asian?

That is the question Asians have to ask themselves. There are Asian doctors, lawyers, judges, engineers, businessmen, scientists, inventors, and so on, but do they know the bigger picture, the issue that's defining them, and how it controls them? Asians are very studious and diligent with their schoolwork and books, and they are scholars from many diverse fields. However, for some reason Asians haven't figured out that they should learn about themselves in America and the rest of the world, how they are portrayed, or what it would take for them to change the way the world views them. This cannot be overlooked, and Asians must break the code to end their stupidity and fully understand how the world operates concerning their roles in mainstream society. Asians should feel a sense of anger beyond their wildest imagination that they have allowed themselves to be fooled for all this time, and nothing has been done about it. With knowledge and education, they should be galvanized to finally do something about their issues.

VI

HOW ASIAN AMERICANS ACQUIRED THESE PROBLEMS

One way Asians acquired these problems was by allowing non-Asians to write about them in biased, disparaging, and condescending ways. In addition, Asians never challenged non-Asians about their writing style, technique, and manipulation of the facts against Asians, which will be presented shortly.

When an Asian American does something wrong, non-Asian writers have a way of linking that person's actions to Asian origins. The writers might say, "This person did something wrong and happens to be a person that has Asian roots." Psychologically, the non-Asian writers are trying to convey to ignorant people that they should hate the Asian person and that person's country and race. The messages are that Asians are devious people, they look different, and they're not part of us. It always goes back to the homeland of the Asian person, pointing to the homeland as the root of a more serious problem. Asians must realize this when reading articles written by non-Asians.

When the oppressors write about an Asian murderer in America, whether an Asian American or Asian, the writer always includes that the murderer is originally from Asian descent. But when a white person commits murder in the United States, that person's European race is seldom discussed. Take, for example, the school shootings of Newtown, Columbine, Virginia Tech, and so many more. We never get the explicit details about the white killer's nationality and country of origin for shootings when the killers are white. But in reports about the shooting at Virginia Tech, we get an incredible amount of information about the race and nationality of the Asian shooter.

The reason why oppressors always write about the Asians' backgrounds is because they want to make the connection that when Asian people do something wrong, it is because their roots are in Asia. The beast wants the world to think that way about Asians.

Furthermore, the oppressors want to treat Asian Americans as though they are not real Americans when compared to white Americans. However, Asians, as well as other groups and nationalities, contributed to the prosperity of America, just like white European Americans. The double standard is obvious. Asians should read articles about Asians more cautiously. I will present two articles in detail to make the point clear.

First let's look at a case about an Asian woman named Annie Le, murdered on September 8, 2009, when her body was stuffed behind a basement wall. She was a student attending Yale University who was killed by an individual who tended mice in the lab. The killer happened to be of European descent, what people of color in America consider a white guy. The *New York Daily News*, a national paper, was very articulate in providing details of how the murder occurred and giving some scenarios of why the white male killed the Asian Yale student. But it never delved into where he was from, where his family came from, or his nationality. Nevertheless, they did a magnificent job describing the victim in the *Daily News*. The article said, "The twenty-four-year-old pharmacology grad student, a California native of Vietnamese descent, went missing last Tuesday." The person who gave me this article pointed out that just by using common sense, you could determine that the woman was an American, because the article stated she was a California native. So why did it mention that she was of Vietnamese descent? Was it trying to say she was American but not *really* American because she was of Asian descent, not white descent, so it was important that they addressed her nationality? Did the article imply the loss of life was not that important because of her Asian descent? What was the reason for the writer including her Asian descent? Would it have been written this way if she were a white woman that was American? Most definitely not! The person who provided me with this article fumed, saying, "You never read an article stating 'A twenty-four-year-old woman was killed, a California native, but her original descent was from Europe,' when it's a country such as Ireland, England, Italy, France, Russia, Scotland, and so forth."

Furthermore, if it were an Asian man who murdered her, you would see a different style of writing—they not only would discuss the murder but also everything about the Asian man's family tree and race. Non-Asian writers who cover stories of Asian incidents always want to correlate Asian people with their race and nationality. It's a way of saying, "This Asian person is no good; all Asians are no good."

Another article is about an Asian student by the name of Seung-Hui Cho, who killed thirty-two innocent individuals on the campus of Virginia Tech: "South Koreans React to Shooting in Virginia" by Choe Sang-Hun and Norimitsu Onishi. This article ran in the *New York Times* on April 18, 2007. Why did South Koreans make an apology to America about the incident? Do all South Koreans feel that they were responsible for the thirty-two students killed? Or could it be because the media blew it up in a way that made it look like one Asian was responsible for all Asians?

The media brilliantly displays one Asian's face and nationality; describes the person as coming from an Asian country, like South Korea; and then correlates that individual's actions to that particular race. When Dylan Klebold and Eric Harris (two whites) slaughtered thirteen students at Colorado's Columbine High School, approximately eight years prior to the Virginia Tech shooting, the newspapers did not go deep into the nationality of the two white individuals. They did not write the stories in such a way that places in Europe, where these individuals originally came from, had to apologize for them.

Writing technique can create prejudice among people. There is definitely a double standard regarding how Asian Americans are written about versus white Americans. The key factor is that the one writing usually is not Asian, so the point of view is very biased, skewed, flawed, and insensitive. To make a long story short, if a lunatic kills someone, what do his parents, grandparents, nationality, and race of origin have to do with it? Nothing. Nonetheless, when writers write about an Asian individual doing something wrong, they create a correlation to that Asian's race and people as a whole. They present it eloquently, without people even seeing the prejudice. It's done with such precision; it cuts out the truth without showing the lie. As stated before, they would not do that to white America; that's the double standard!

To make the point further, when Cho killed thirty-two students at Virginia Tech, writers put an Asian face to the crime. So people came to hate the Asian look. Writers continued to write about Cho's origin, causing readers to hate South Koreans. The press then displayed the Asian face in various ways, so the readers hated the whole Asian race. It's simple, methodical, mathematical, psychological brilliance. An Asian person did wrong; therefore, all Asians do wrong. They say it many times and employ creative tactics, utilizing the media.

They use this technique with everything: China is communist, and they don't want to give you your freedom. Chinese people are Asians; all Asians don't want to give you your freedom. Hate all Asians. Understand the way of the words, and then you can read between the lines.

Seung-Hui Cho had been in America for approximately fifteen years, based on the article; therefore, he was already indoctrinated in the American way. He practically grew up in America. Why did writers need to identify his origin and make it seem that because he was Korean or Asian, he was crazy? For most white murderers, writers don't identify their nationality of origin; everyone in America immigrated here, except for American Indians. In the case of white European American murderers, such as serial killers, gangsters, and so forth, writers only stick to the crimes and don't really go into depth about white criminals' original nationalities. It's not necessary, and one's nationality does not have anything to do with a person's crime, but non-Asian writers have a way of correlating the two when it comes to Asian murderers. This is extreme prejudice.

The oppressors use the Pavlovian psychological technique when portraying Asians. A dog will salivate when he hears the tuning fork, believing it signals food. Oppressors correlate Asians with criminals or wrongdoers. After using this technique enough times, they cause non-Asians to believe that Asians are not good. The technique is simple and powerful and uses various media outlets to further the myth. They do this because "whenever one group of people is taught to hate another, a lie is created to inflame the hatred and justify a plot," as writer Will Eisner said. This is where the stereotype begins, and it permeates forever, unless Asians wake up and stop it. Asians must be aware and on the lookout.

When this occurs through various media, Asians need to address the problem.

As stated before, a powerful psychological technique and the phenomenon of prejudice appear when observing all the writings about Asians by non-Asians, from the beginning of time. Look out for it. It has profound, deadly consequences for Asians. If Asians don't consciously notice and address it, holding accountable those who use this technique, the plots to destroy all Asians will continue. This is only one story from a collection of many about how non-Asians write about Asian Americans. It's important that Asians research and gather the numerous articles of the past century written about Asian Americans, as well as Asians abroad, and observe the writing technique and how it is biased against Asians.

Another reason these problems came about is that Asian Americans are a very silent voice in American society. Asians in modern society are sometimes virtually invisible and soft-spoken. Because of that, they are not exposing themselves to the world as human beings. Therefore, non-Asians can easily portray Asians as subhuman, without any feelings, and not part of their society. Asians are looked at as people that could not assimilate because they didn't involve themselves in regular, everyday life. This leads some people to think they can depict Asians however they please, without recourse. It's hard for non-Asians to take Asians seriously when Asians are not a major factor or influence in society; therefore, Asians have to be very vocal, become more involved, and force their influence on mainstream society.

Asian Americans are a small percentage of the population in America, and this has contributed to the problems discussed earlier. Asians in America are only about 4.8 percent of the people in the United States as of 2014. It's a small portion compared to white America, black America, or Hispanic America. Given Asian Americans are relatively small in number, they do not have enough voting constituents to influence elective officials to cater to their needs and wants. Therefore, some businesses, politicians, and non-Asian individuals overlook the Asian American groups, because of the small population numbers. Nonetheless, you can have a small base but still be powerful and influential, as Jewish Americans are. For example, it's common knowledge that Jewish Americans pretty much own and control the media, as well as many other things in America. To get the facts about it, all you have to do is a Google search. There are numerous articles, such as "Jewish Dominance of America—Facts Are Facts," by Jonathan Silverman. You'll get educated about the influence, power, and control that Jewish Americans wield. However, Jewish Americans are only about 2.2 percent of the American population as of 2014, based on information from jewishvir-tuallibrary.org. Thus, Jewish Americans are able to portray their people and race on all media channels. It takes intelligence, perseverance, and unity to achieve recognition and control with a small percentage in the American population. The Jewish people have figured it out brilliantly.

Given that Asian Americans are approximately 4.8 percent of the American population, and not white like Jewish people, their circumstance is somewhat different. It's difficult to convince non-Asians to think about the concerns of Asians when their population in America is low. However, if Asian Americans utilized the Asian population worldwide, Asians would have astronomical power, because worldwide they make up a larger percentage of the population than any other race. Asians should not be overlooked. There's serious power in numbers, and there are billions of Asians, but Asians don't utilize this. In later chapters, we will discuss more about Asian unity.

Another factor contributing to the development of these problems is that Asian Americans overlook the "grand ol' scheme." This means that the beast psychologically plays mind games and convinces Asian Americans to hate Asians abroad by using the media to make them feel un-American. When Asian Americans disagree with foreign policies, the beast tries to portray Asian Americans as un-American. For example, when Asian Americans voiced that they were against the Vietnam War, white America accused them of being un-American. Other groups of Americans are not concerned with Asian American issues, so only American Asians can bring out those issues, just like African Americans can for African American issues. Asians have to realize it's propaganda, know how it's played, and fight it. They need to do a better job to organize their numerous groups and to inform Asians about the concerns that affect them. To combat the beast, Asians should write articles for numerous media outlets to educate people about how the oppressors play their games against Asians.

Ultimately, the beast has devised a plan to make American Asians hate America by oppressing and discriminating against them. It is called forced incarceration. In America, for example, the oppressor can jail, discriminate, oppress, and do many unrighteous things to Asians, forcing them to break the law by challenging it. Once Asians break the law, due to the injustice, the beast can turn around and accuse the Asians of being criminals and lawbreakers.

As stated earlier, some oppressors make Asian Americans feel as though they're not Americans at all. Yet it was the oppressors who first utilized certain unconstitutional policies against Asians that caused the hatred in the first place. After Japan bombed Pearl Harbor during World War II, white America detained Japanese Americans in camps, accusing them of being spies and traitors. If Japanese Americans refused to be detained in the camps, they were breaking the law. Those unconstitutional actions caused Japanese Americans to have animosity against white Americans, who made those unlawful policies in the first place. Nevertheless, America didn't arrest and detain all German and Italian Americans, accusing them of being traitors, because Hitler was German and Mussolini was Italian. Double standard and bias? Of course. If the oppressors have their minds set on convicting you as an Asian, no matter how innocent or right you may be, they will use all their resources and conjure up any reason to do it, even if it's fundamentally wrong.

Thus, it is inevitable that Asians will repeat the past, which means unlawful detainment of Asian Americans. Asian Americans must be more united and more vocal in the United States if they do not want history to repeat itself. Just imagine if the United States were to go to war with China because China declared war with Taiwan or if the United States went to war with North Korea because North Korea declared war with South Korea. White America might round up every Korean and Chinese American and accuse them of being traitors without due process and send them straight to detention camps, like they did to Japanese Americans in World War II. In addition, any war that an Asian country gets involved in will be accompanied by propaganda made by the beast. It will be designed to make others hate all types of Asians and orchestrated throughout various mediums, stereotyping and portraying Asians as dishonorable people.

Complacency! When at peace, sometimes Asians feel safe in their current situation and are able to talk and rationalize past actions taken against them. Thus, Asians don't do anything unless it's too late, and then they find themselves in a panicked state. Therefore, it's best to let Asians think of what they will do if they are in a particular situation, like a state of emergency, so that they take it more seriously. For example, the Japanese Americans during peacetime, before World War II, were all very complacent and tranquil, feeling safe. But when World War II occurred and Japan bombed Pearl Harbor, Japanese Americans were rounded up and deported to an isolated place in America. During World War

II, Japanese Americans were stripped of their rights, dignity, and property. Thus, Asian Americans should always imagine themselves in that actual place and time. Asians should never be complacent but should prepare well in advance what they will do when they again are denigrated at times of injustice—when the oppressors humiliate them.

The main point is that Asian Americans should get together to make sure that unrighteous things, like what happened to the Japanese Americans, don't happen again in the future. Asian should never be complacent; they should think of their sovereignty and livelihood at all times and fight at any sudden signs that unrighteousness may come along again. Asians now have to challenge and question policies that affect them. Asian Americans have to involve themselves with the political system in the United States before such injustice recurs.

Another problem for Asian Americans is that some Asians don't realize that time is extremely important. Asians don't intelligently segment their time. On the contrary, some Asians continue to watch the oppressors' activities through entertainment, TV, movies, and sports, and they waste their valuable time and money without having lives of their own. Asians have to educate the next generation of Asians to be more knowledgeable of how the world works and how it affects them.

Asians don't look at the importance of the ticking clock. Every year, month, day, hour, minute, and second will count for Asians. If Asians continue to watch racist non-Asian activities and fall prey to them, then this will prove to be unproductive and deadly, as Asian holocaust could commence. This would be similar to what happened with the Jews in Germany while the Nazis prepared to dispose of them. The Jews weren't prepared for the Nazi plan for their elimination. It took years for Hitler to plan his ruthless attacks. Some may argue that when he was feeding hatred to his people against Jews, maybe the world should have took his rhetoric more seriously early on to prevent his actions. Time is pivotal; like certain diseases, if you pinpoint a problem in its early stages, you could treat it and hopefully cure it. If you let time pass by, and it's too late, you could die. Some think that if the world had taken notice of Hitler's hateful speeches in the beginning, maybe it would have been easier for the world and his people to take him out of office, cutting short his power—and preventing the Holocaust.

Asians should never find themselves in the same or similar predicament as those in the Jewish Holocaust.

Asians must be alert and urgent about the issues. If Asian Americans don't prepare now, with a sense of emergency, as time is ticking, it will give the oppressors ample time to gather their resources and bring Asians down again. They will then enslave them and demoralize them as a people. Therefore, Asians must be aware and always analyze the rhetoric of politicians and political figures anywhere in the world speaking negatively about Asians, and take actions now rather than later to resolve any issues that need to be addressed.

Another factor contributing to the development of these problems is that Asian Americans never challenge white Americans about who is considered American.

Everyone who's truly knowledgeable about history will acknowledge that the Native Americans were the first people who roamed the land that we call America. However, after the European people arrived, they conquered the Indian people, committed genocide, and didn't want to accept the simple fact that they are immigrants themselves. The Europeans devised a manipulative, complicated, and complex plan to rewrite history or tweak it. They stated that Christopher Columbus, a European, discovered America. They tried to establish a new history stating that the white European people were always here in America, and everyone else who is non-European is an immigrant. It was a brilliant contortion of facts, and if you believe it, then you are the biggest fool.

If it were the other way around, and Native Americans came to Europe in a boat and decided to say they discovered and conquered Europe, I don't believe the Europeans would accept that part of history. European Americans, better known as white Americans, did a splendid job convincing the world that an American is a person who is white. Those who don't know any better and are ignorant about the history of how America was created believe this.

This is because the history of America was written from the point of view of European immigrants for the benefit of European whites that would soon be Americans. If the oppressors could convince the ignorant that they were the true natives, and no one existed before them in this land called America, then they could consider everyone else as immigrants—that was the ultimate goal! The Europeans could make the rules in their favor with no one to fight them. This means that some white Europeans living in America consider Asian Americans as immigrants, when they themselves are immigrants as well.

The bottom line is that oppressors will always use manipulative, unethical, and immoral reasoning to justify their wrongs and achieve their outcome instead of using simple, correct common sense.

During World War II, Germans and Italians were living in America. They were considered Americans and wanted to be viewed as separate from their countrymen in Italy or Germany, who were against America during the war. These German Americans and Italian Americans wanted to be thought of as Americans, not as Germans from Hitler's Germany or Italians from Mussolini's Italy.

In America, white individuals who originated in Europe like to be referred to by where they grew up within the fifty states of America. For example, if a white individual grew up in New York, that person likes to be referred to as a New Yorker.

White European people who grew up in America do not like to be referred to as a Swedish American, German American, Irish American, Australian American, European American, and so on. They want to be referred to as "American," or by the state where they grew up in America, but when it comes to Asian Americans who grew up in America, white Americans like to refer to them by their original Asian descent. They find it difficult to refer to Asians who grew up in the United States as just "American," even though their circumstances are very similar to white European people who immigrated to America.

Thus, when it comes to Asians in America, white America wants to view Asian Americans as enemies from abroad. They do not want to differentiate Asian Americans differently from other Asians, like they do with white European Americans. This is the reason Japanese Americans were sent to detention camps in World War II. White Americans viewed Japanese Americans, raised in America, as if they were Japanese people from Japan fighting against America in World War II.

Here's another example: Irish Americans don't want to be affiliated with the Irish Republican Army in Ireland, fighting against Great Britain. The Irish people in America want to be thought of as American. Irish Americans want to be separated from that group.

However, when it comes to Asians, some white oppressors want to affiliate them with their countrymen and associate them with the negatives instead of treating them as full Americans. To illustrate the point further, when something happens in an Asian country, non-Asians in America ask stupid questions about how Asian Americans feel about the situation, as if all Asian Americans only arrived in America a few seconds ago from the boat. The oppressors do this to try to make Asians who grew up in America feel as if they are not real Americans because of the color of their skin and the slant of their eyes. The beast wants to focus on the negative side and doesn't allow Asians to belong to a greater organization like America, which was built by numerous people of various color, not only the selected white European oppressors who control America. Oppressors always try to link Asian Americans to their Asian descendants back in their countries, but white European Americans are never referred to with regard to their original countries in Europe. There will always be a double standard, and Asians have to take notice of it and address it.

As mentioned earlier, the beast manipulates the truth. Falling for these manipulations has helped create the issues that Asians face today. Smart, educated, devious people, like the oppressors, sometimes make an easy thing complicated. What is simple becomes confusing and complex. When you see really educated people going to brilliant schools, they try to go up and beyond, and they don't take the easy road but the more difficult one. Thus, their manipulated reasoning is flawed, and if they twist it brilliantly, they can use their knowledge to confuse you and complicate the situation in order to trick and fool you. This is why many Asians are fooled.

For example, everyone knows murder is wrong, and if you commit it, you should be punished and prosecuted for it. However, for some reason, when innocent Vincent Chin was killed for being Asian, which was definitively wrong, the oppressors figured out a way to escape prosecution. They manufactured a complicated, manipulative, complex reason for allowing the oppressor who murdered an Asian to be set free.

A second example is that everyone knows that you need to follow "due process," before taking people's rights and liberties away from them. Nonetheless, when Japanese Americans were rounded up, sent to detention camps, and accused of being traitors during World War II, the oppressors used an unconstitutional, confusing, manipulative reasoning to incarcerate Asians without due process.

Another element contributing to Asian American issues is that some Asian Americans, because of many years of suppression by the oppressors, have that "I'd rather kill myself" mentality. They just deal with it, similar to how domestic-abuse victims behave. This means being soft and not fighting the issues concerning them, accepting abuse from the three categories of oppressors. This leads to self-inflicted damage due to extremely low self-esteem; they let everyone step all over them. Take, for example, Private Danny Chen, a Chinese American soldier who committed suicide because he was taunted by racist nicknames, ordered by his non-Asian sergeant to belly crawl over rocks, and made to bark out orders in Chinese to give the non-Asian platoon a laugh. In addition, his army sergeant, Andrew Van Bockel, allowed other soldiers to torture Chen by beating him up, throwing rocks at him, and forcing him to do push-ups with a mouthful of water. If Asians suddenly decided to change their "I'd rather kill myself" mentality, then Private Chen should have taken his gun and shot those disrespecting him, in the name of self-defense.

There are Asians who, sadly, accept society because "that is the way it is." They choose not to do anything, and the life of bullshit becomes their own, at their own pathetic expense. Some Asians don't mind standing on quicksand with their mouths duct-taped as they slowly sink into nothingness, the way the oppressors or beast planned it to be. Some Asians don't look at their concerns as serious and consider them somewhat laughable.

However, as days go on, Asians will eventually see how they are being ridiculed on a daily basis; then they will realize what fools they are for not getting involved with Asian causes. Hopefully those Asians will not be too late to get involved, because a hidden holocaust may be near for Asians if they continue to do nothing.

The way Asians should view how they are mistreated is to ask whether the beast would accept the same disrespect that Asians endure and experience. If the inequality were reversed, would the beast accept the same abuse? The answer is simply *no*. Thus, why should Asians accept disrespect?

The desire for approval has also contributed to Asian Americans' problems. As stated previously, some Asian Americans try so hard to be accepted by white Americans— trying to imitate the way they speak, with the same diction and accent—that they forget their own language and culture. These Asian Americans are really trying to imitate and become white people. It has nothing to do with the English language itself. African Americans also use the English language, but they developed their own style of English to cater to their own race and culture. Asians have to do the same and make their own style of English. In other words, just be your own person. Don't try to follow someone else to a tee and eventually morph into a Twinkie or coconut, which will ultimately betray the Asian cause. For an Asian to forget oneself just to find "acceptance" from another group is like a wife being beaten by her husband, and allowing it to continue, only to keep the abusive relationship going.

Some Asians listen to music, love it, and overlook the lyrics, not understanding that the words are sometimes used to kill them. I know of an Asian individual who loved a particular song and had no idea what the lyrics of the song really meant until he saw the printed version. Bruce Springsteen is a godlike icon in music; he has millions of fans. In the song "Born in the USA," he sings, "Sent me off to a foreign land, to go and kill the yellow man." Everyone who listens, loves it, justifying that killing an Asian is acceptable. However, if it said he'd gone to Somalia (also a foreign land) to go and kill the black man, there would be a riots and protests. But because Asians don't dispute it, the song is an ultimate, golden, classic hit.

On a personal note, I don't believe Bruce Springsteen is prejudiced, or I hope he's not. I actually like his music and persona. But after someone pointed out the lyrics to "Born in the USA," I feel that his choice of words on that particular song could have been different.

The main point is to show that whether it's through TV, movies, music, or newspapers, these various mediums are used to denigrate and advocate hate for Asians.

Another contributing factor is that Asian Americans are not attentive when oppressors display token Asians at the front line to the world, contradicting Asian movements for equality and disputing the fact that oppressors are prejudiced against Asian people. Always keep in mind that token Asians are very few.

For example, when you see some Asian broadcasters on news networks, Asian actors in films, or Asian executives in non-Asian firms, you might believe that Asians are progressing and moving up in mainstream society. But don't be fooled, because some of those Asians really are puppets on a string, set up and controlled by oppressors. Some of those Asians you see on the front line are actually Twinkies or coconuts. This is what you would consider a "sheep in wolf's clothing." Some of these token Asians are utilized to imply that Asians are not discriminated against and are on equal terms with everyone, but real Asians should be smarter than that. Token Asians are displayed as fake showcases to undermine the Asian cause. Oppressors use token Asians to show the world that Asians are doing OK and that there are no such things as Asian issues, but don't believe it.

Lack of representation contributes to the problems Asians face. Asian people do not have a Martin Luther King Jr., Malcolm X, Frederick Douglass, or Nelson Mandela to speak about issues that concern them. A revolution must begin, and there must be more activists and leaders in Asian communities.

VII

How Asians Abroad Acquired
these Problems

There are many obstacles and reasons why Asians are not united globally. Asians from various countries have language barriers, cultural differences, and bad history among themselves, unlike people from Spanish or Hispanic descent, who have similarities in their language. When a Spanish-speaking person from Puerto Rico goes to South or Central America, or Spain, he or she can communicate with the people because the Spanish language is similar. In contrast, a Korean can't go to China or Japan and speak Korean to communicate. The language barrier does become an obstacle with Asians. In addition to the cultural differences, World War II animosity among Asians creates disunity.

Asians were not the first to venture into certain key global markets. In business this is called brand recognition. The later you enter certain markets, the harder it is to compete with things that are already established. A strong brand name and image offer an organization several important advantages. The brand name distinguishes a product from competitors' products. A powerful brand identity creates a major competitive advantage. A brand that is recognized by buyers encourages repeat purchases.

Some Asian countries unwisely decided in the past to be self-sufficient and block their people from the world. This hurt their competitive edge as well as their ability to obtain broad, global, essential knowledge from other people. To compete worldwide, Asians need to fully know what the trends of mainstream societies in the entire world are and to understand what people like or dislike globally, what sells, and what doesn't. In the case of some Asian countries, they were a little late to enter certain industries in mainstream society, such as music and films that attract international attention, which is the reason non-Asian people don't buy Asian records or watch Asian films.

However, it's still not too late to dominate the markets. If Asians back up their fellow singers, musicians, and actors, and those artists become more innovative and diverse in their art, bringing Asians into mainstream society could be achieved. Furthermore, Asians should back up and encourage Asians to go seek out other industries that they are not known for.

Another problem is the lack of innovation from Asian countries. When China first invented gunpowder, they didn't take it to the next level and make innovative, effective guns to utilize it. It was Europe that took it to the next level by using the gunpowder and making guns to use in war. There are a lot of opinions from Asians about why China didn't advance in weapons innovation using the gunpowder. Maybe China didn't want to invent an item that would soon kill mankind, or maybe the culture at the time didn't allow their minds to think in a warlike fashion. Whatever the assumption, this became a detriment to Asians. Non-Asian countries took the gunpowder idea, invented the perfect gun, and used it against Asian countries. So the moral of the story is that Asians have to think of innovative ways to help improve their self-preservation and national interest, so they can defend and protect themselves in the future. Asians should never think that the oppressors are not already planning to commit a complete genocide on them.

What happened to cause some Asian countries to end up as third-world countries? Some Asians assumed that these Asian countries became lazy and unmotivated, and there's a theory behind it. In the very beginning, before people from each individual country ventured into other countries and explored, every individual country in the entire world started out the same, trying to survive in their own land of origin with whatever resources they had. And some Asian countries were fortunate and blessed to have tropical, warm climates. People living there were happy in jungles, with an abundance of food from fruits, vegetables, livestock, fishes, and all the animals around them. Therefore, Asian people living in these paradises could be lazy, because their countries had resources that allowed them to be self-sufficient.

They had great weather, natural resources, gold, minerals, and so much more.

They didn't really have to struggle much for their essentials. These Asian inhabitants didn't need to venture onto other continents to obtain their basic needs. They were peaceful and lived in tranquility. This became their doom, because these Asians were not thinking about their national security and their military. But people from other lands, such as Europe, who didn't have the resources or privileges of these Asian lands, were looking for these items. When Spain, France, and other countries in Europe planned to conquer these Asian countries. The inhabitants of these Asian countries had fun all day and slept all night; they hadn't built their security to the fullest and couldn't protect themselves from pirates ready to attack and take their lifestyle away from them. The moral of the story is that Asians should not be lazy, complacent, unknowledgeable, and unmotivated. It's essential for every Asian country to learn from its mistakes and start being proactive in building security and prosperity. Non-Asian oppressors or even neighboring Asians countries won't be able to take what they've got, when they least expect it, and make them slaves and paupers. It's very similar to the Native Americans' story.

Another problem for Asians abroad is that third-world countries such as Thailand, Vietnam, Malaysia, the Philippines, Indonesia, and so forth, gave opportunities for the oppressors to denigrate the race. White Europeans and white Americans found a way to profit from underage Asian children, disgracefully using them as prostitutes and sex slaves. The oppressors hypocritically like to preach morals and God to their own people but use a different standard for uneducated, helpless Asian youngsters. Unfortunately, Asian leaders allowed this for the sole purpose of money. Nevertheless, the long-term effect was devastating and still affects these countries. Third-world Asian countries have no idea how foolish they look to non-Asian industrial countries.

It's up to these Asian countries to understand what's going on, so they can change it and stop the disrespect and disparagement of their people that's been going on far too long.

Neglecting females' education has also contributed to the problems of Asians abroad. It is the responsibility of Asian world leaders to implement and facilitate education for their people, particularly young, innocent, naïve, uneducated girls, so they are not denigrated. Many non-Asian foreigners come to Asia to take advantage of these opportunities. Many Asian females, particularly young, benighted, naïve, innocent girls, think non-Asians who come from abroad will become their providers and saviors, only to realize they have been fooled. In fact, some Asian girls who see non-Asian people for the first time are excited, because of what they see in the media, thinking that all non-Asians are good people. However, sometimes they get taken advantage of and find out the hard way, when it's too late. This excitement comes from inexperience and ignorance. Uneducated Asian females are the oppressor's dream. Sometimes you have non-Asian losers who couldn't get a partner in their own country, or criminals, or extremely old people, who go to these Asian countries to marry very young, naïve Asian kids. Unfortunately, some uneducated Asians in the third world countries are so vulnerable, that they essentially sell their own children to get their basic needs. It is immensely important that all Asian individuals globally are educated, so they don't fall into the trap of "ultimate slavery." Uneducated females being taking advantage of due to ignorance is the fault of these particular Asian countries' governments.

Andrea Jung and Vera Wang are two strong, intelligent Asian women who showcase the difference between smart Asian women and the unfortunate, uneducated ones. Andrea Jung is an executive, a nonprofit leader, and a prominent women's issues supporter. In April 2014, she became president and CEO of Grameen America, a nonprofit microfinance organization. From 1999 until 2012, she served as the first female CEO and chairman of Avon Products, Inc. She was also the first woman to serve as chairman of the Cosmetic, Toiletry, and Fragrance Association and chairman of the World Federation of Direct Selling Associations. In addition, Andrea Jung is a magna cum laude graduate of Princeton University, an Ivy League college.

Vera Wang is a world-renowned fashion designer based in New York City and former figure skater. Wang was a former senior fashion editor for *Vogue* and joined Ralph Lauren as a design director for two years. Wang has made wedding gowns for many well-known public figures and has designed costumes for numerous top figure skaters.

These two successful women are presented to make an extreme point: they would not bow down and shine the shoes of or be overly impressed by a non-Asian person, whether the individual was white, black, Hispanic, or another ethnicity. The reason is because Andrea Jung and Vera Wang are two Asian women that are educated, sophisticated, and knowledgeable about how the world works. They don't look down on themselves as Asian women to please non-Asian people. Many Asian women abroad, especially in third-world, underdeveloped countries, think non-Asian people are heaven-sent. Their minds are conditioned to be like those of slaves, and they're willing to do anything to please non-Asians. They treat non-Asian people like royalty and end up selling their souls to them.

The main point is to separate the two ways of thinking. On one side, you have educated Asian women, such as Andrea Jung and Vera Wang, who don't allow people to disrespect them, because they're classy, educated, and experienced. On the other side, many gullible, uneducated Asian women have such low self-esteem that they allow non-Asian people to take advantage of them, because of their lack of knowledge, experience, and education.

The question to ask any Asian woman is, which one are you?

These two successful women above may be exceptional; however, there are other Asian women who may not be as successful as Andrea or Vera but also know the issues and don't denigrate themselves. God bless them as well.

It is incumbent for government officials in Asian countries to implement aggressive, crucial programs to educate all Asian individuals who may not be capable of obtaining higher education or knowledge due to economic setbacks. Asian countries have to realize that investing in education for their people will bring a much higher return of success for their country. Asian countries do not want to breed a race of people who are uneducated and stupid, because those individuals won't improve their country. If Asian leaders, particular in third-world countries, don't provide easy access to higher education for their people, they face total annihilation. Their people and country will lack advancement from technology, medicine, innovation, military, political stability, and so much more. They will not have the right human backup they need to progress in a highly competitive world. These Asian leaders must realize they need their own people to succeed as a team.

Asians are not fully aware that a weapon of mass destruction was only used on them. The atom bomb was used only against the Asian people; it has been used against no other race. Thus, Asians should realize how much the oppressors hated Asian people. Some Asians never discuss and question why the atom bomb was never used in any other country. Was a bomb of mass destruction necessary, given that Japan was already losing the war? The Asian haters don't care about the Asian people, and Asians should embrace that reality, accept it, and work with it.

Asians from the Pacific didn't learn from the past. Imperial Japan, during World War II, decided to disrespect its Asian neighbors, then conquer and occupy them. These Asian countries, with the exception of China and North Korea, did not learn from it. Asian countries today must all acquire nuclear arsenals to protect their sovereignty and national interest, so they are not conquered again and humiliated like they were in the past. Asian leaders have to realize that working with their people, not stealing from them or enslaving them, will make them prosper. Unity is power, and working together will strengthen Asian countries from within.

Now that I've presented the vast problems that both Asian Americans and Asians abroad face, I will provide more concrete history from various sources. Asians everywhere gave me these sources to confirm and back up their stories.

VIII

STORIES VOICED BY REAL ASIANS, AND FACTS PROVIDED TO BACK THEM UP

I will now provide a collection of numerous Asian stories from everyday Asians to reinforce the fact that Asians are discriminated against, and everything is not fine concerning Asian issues.

I asked many Asians from various ethnicities to explain to me Asian issues and to provide solid facts to back up their stories. These are articles that prove the dilemma Asians face. Of the Asian people I interviewed for this book, I only wrote the opinions of those who could provide me with solid facts and hard evidence.

I will first present stories and articles that are all true but were given to me without known dates, because the Asian individuals didn't accurately record them, or forgot. With further research, I'm sure the dates of these stories could actually be captured, but because of exhaustive time, effort, and laziness, I decided not to obtain them. In the second section, I will present stories and articles for which I do have actual dates and documented resources.

THE FIRST IS A STORY FROM A JAPANESE ASIAN AMERICAN:

It was some time ago when *Details* magazine featured an issue showing a photo of an Asian man accompanied by text and arrows pointing at the different parts of his body. The headline was "Gay or Asian?" The magazine could have been implying many things, such as Asian men were gay or wore clothes that made them look gay or that their body parts made them gay. There were a lot of potential misinterpretations about the picture, because a picture can say a thousand words. The magazine chose to display Asians because Asians were known to be peaceful, passive, and nonconfrontational, so it was easy to poke fun at Asians without worry of recourse.

Luckily, a Harvard University sophomore by the name of Sarah Paiji arranged for a busload of college students to attend a protest. She stated, "We're sick of the media telling us who we are. We're taking a stand." She was, without doubt, a very brave individual to do this. More Asians, if not all Asians, absolutely must take a stand and be as courageous as she was. Thus, whenever Asians hear, see, or read a story that belittles Asians, they must take a stand and seek necessary actions to end it.

Only Asian Americans should define what an Asian American is, just like African Americans and Latino or Hispanic

Americans don't allow white Americans or anyone else to define what they are. When it comes to Asians, it is an Asian thing—non-Asians wouldn't understand.

ANOTHER STORY IS FROM A TAIWANESE ASIAN AMERICAN:

Non-Asians have a way of making Asians feel like fools. Take, for example, *American Idol*, once one of the most popular shows in America. In the show's third season, an Asian person by the name of William Hung auditioned, and he obviously wasn't the best singer in the world, but non-Asians saw it as an opportunity to disrespect Asians. They made albums with him and gave him a stage to perform on for the world to see, not because they thought he was a great singer or performer but because it was an opportunity to make fun of him. They hoped it would resonate to making fun of all Asians, because William Hung was Asian and looked Asian. And if any Asians wished to be singers, the beast could refer to them similarly to William Hung. Do you see how the oppressors work? If it goes over your head, then you go with the flow, but if you're smart, you'll see how the game is played.

A STORY FROM A KOREAN ASIAN AMERICAN:

According to a *Daily News* article, Kevin Kim was a candidate running for nineteenth district city council in Queens. His opponent, Republican Dan Halloran, used a brilliant scare tactic to win votes—the race issue. Some people believed that Dan Halloran couldn't win by his record alone. Halloran was white, and Kim was Asian, and the district was still predominately white. So Halloran painted Kim as an "outsider," even though Kim, a Korean American, grew up in the area. It didn't matter that Kim was quintessentially American; if Halloran could convince the voters that Asian people were "foreigners," though he instead used the word "outsider," he knew what it would mean in white people's minds. The Asians that supported Kevin Kim stated that Halloran knew there was still a great amount of white voters who were prejudiced, and those votes counted. Therefore, Halloran won. An article titled "Embattled Halloran Could Pave Way for Return of Old Rival" by Stella Chan appeared on www.voicesofny.org on April 10, 2013. Sourced from the *Sing Tao Daily*, Chan wrote, "Halloran managed to turn the tide with shocking campaign strategies. For example, his campaign handed out campaign flyers with a picture of crowds of new immigrants on the streets in neighboring Flushing, captioned 'Do you want Bayside to be like this?'" In the same article: "Furthermore, according to a complaint filed to the US Department of Justice (DOJ) by the Asian American Legal Defense and Education Fund (AALDEF) in 2010, Kim's campaign workers were attacked and experienced discrimination. The NYPD has also investigated a case in which a group of young white men attacked two volunteers of Kim's campaign and shouted racist phrases like "white power!" and "white supremacy!" Apparently, during the melee, a Korean volunteer was injured in the head. Another article appeared in the *Daily News* by Lisa L. Colangelo on August 24, 2012 titled "Queens Congress Race Gets Nasty—and Racial." The Asians who provided the article felt the tactics Halloran utilized to win the election could be interpreted as racist.

The reasoning behind this is that the general public is still not comfortable with Asians as elected officials. One reason is because Asians are seldom seen in the media with a personality. Thus, it is easier for the oppressors to depict them as anything they please. Given that Asians are always hidden from the spotlight, they must come out and become very aggressive, with no fear, so that they can break the stereotype that people have of them.

THE FOLLOWING IS A STORY PROVIDED TO ME BY A CHINESE ASIAN AMERICAN:

A Chinese-food deliveryman, Fengwang Chen, was shot in the head in the Bronx. The bullet entered behind his ear and lodged in his jaw. He was married and the father of two young children.

In another situation, a fourteen-year-old suspect (of non-Asian descent) punched a twenty-four-year-old Columbia University student named Minghui Yu, from China. The punch sent Yu fleeing into traffic, where a jeep hit and killed him. Yu was a talented scholar and graduate student.

What is the moral of all these stories? Asians are looked at as perfect, easy victims. That is why they are prowled against; this is the reason Asians have to change the perception.

THIS STORY IS FROM A CAMBODIAN ASIAN AMERICAN:

The US Army killed South Vietnamese civilians in the infamous episode known as the My Lai Massacre. This is a great example of a non-Asian army killing innocent Asians. Imagine it the other way around, and Asian soldiers went to Europe to take sides with an indifferent political system. Imagine if they decided to kill innocent white people and left them on the road just for the hell of it. Would that be acceptable?

Non-Asians should never meddle in the business of Asian squabbles. The situation is similar to a family trying to settle its own business. As another example, just imagine an Asian country going into the United States during the Civil War and taking sides with either the Confederate or Union army and, along the way, raping and murdering innocent American inhabitants. How would Asians be written about in history? Well, this was happening in Vietnam; there was a civil war between the North and South Vietnamese, and the United States got involved and massacred and raped innocent Vietnamese people along the way.

Here is a story from a Burmese Asian American historian:

The Chinese ship *Golden Venture* landed on the shore off Far Rockaway, Queens, New York, sometime in the summer of 1993. It could have easily been said that those Asian refugees discovered America, but how many white Europeans would buy that story? However, wasn't that the way Christopher Columbus did it? We are taught and educated by European, white writers that Columbus discovered America, and white America agree, without realizing the Native Americans were already here. The historian commented, "You can't discover something that people already know about." It's all about thought manipulation, and those who do become enslaved by ignorance and stupidity are those that will fall down to their knees, begging like peasants. Those gullible people are also the ones that don't advance to bigger and more prosperous futures because of their ignorance.

The next story is from a Thai Asian American cook:

This Thai cook read an article in a daily paper about Chinese or Asian restaurant food. The news article described how fattening Asian foods are because of the grease content. The cook was furious about the story, because as a chef, he made many Asian dishes. He stated that of course there were some Asian dishes that were fattening, just like some dishes of every ethnicity, but to generalize and make the assumption that

Asian food in general caused people to become fat was flawed, absurd, and made absolutely "*no* sense." The Thai cook pointed out that if Asian food was so fattening, then look around the world or in the big cities—Asian people, for the most part, are not fatter than non-Asian people. In fact, it's the other way around; Asian people are skinnier than most non-Asian people. The Thai cook believes the non-Asian writer went national on this story, hoping people would be discouraged from eating Asian food from restaurants. Then the Asian food market and Asian restaurants would lose their market share and plummet downward while non-Asian restaurants prospered.

Furthermore, the non-Asian writer introduced an Asian individual in the article, who was supposed to be a professional of some sort about the topic. The Asian expert was used to confirm the claim that Asian food was fattening. This was a brilliant technique used by the non-Asian writer, to validate his opinion just in case a backlash rose against him. The non-Asian writer could use the Asian expert as a scapegoat.

This technique is also used in films. When non-Asian writers depict Asians as fools, you will also see Asian writers credited in the films. Non-Asian writers do this to convince you that Asians also collaborated in writing these movies that made Asians look like dorks. Asians should not fall for this clever technique.

THIS STORY COMES FROM A CHINESE VISITOR:
During the Bush administration, an American spy plane flew over China, hoping to investigate what China was up to. The

American spy plane collided with a Chinese fighter jet, and the spy plane was forced to land on the Chinese island of Hainan.

When all was said and done, the American crew members on the spy plane were allowed to return back to the United States safely, as a humanitarian gesture. The American crew members were greeted with applause and celebration.

The question is, what if it were the other way around, and a Chinese spy plane flew over America? What would be the negative ramifications? Would the white European portion of America release the Chinese crew members back to China as a humanitarian gesture or keep them detained?

I tried to remember the long conversation I had with the Chinese visitor; the main point of his argument was that some countries always want to view Chinese people as spies, engaging in suspicious activities like cyberattacks, espionage, and such, but not realizing that other countries are doing those things to China. Again, notice the double standard as describe by the visitor.

IX

Now I will present more true stories, in chronological order, with documented dates and the resource of origin. First, I will provide evidence given to me by Asian Americans. Then I will provide proof given to me by Asians abroad, not Asian Americans.

Every Asian who's truly involved with Asian issues is familiar with the "Who Killed Vincent Chin?" story. The story is about a Chinese American who was killed by two white Americans in June 1982. Vincent Chin was out trying to have fun before he got married. He decided to have a good time spending his limited bachelorhood at a topless bar. During the evening, he got into a confrontation with two customers—Ron Ebens, an unemployed (white American) auto worker, and Michael Nitz, Ron's stepson. The two white

Americans left the topless bar and later came back for Mr. Chin. Surprisingly, Vincent Chin's friends—including white American friends—and strangers looked on as Mr. Nitz held Mr. Chin while Mr. Ebens beat him over the head with a baseball bat.

Ronald Ebens had decided to beat up a Chinese American who he thought was Japanese. Apparently, overseas Japanese carmakers had recently created unwanted competition that forced American automakers to lay off many workers in America.

The shocking part is that Ronald Ebens, a white American, killed a young Chinese American engineer with a baseball bat and never served jail time, even though he undeniably confessed to the murder.

In fact, in one of Mr. Ebens's interviews, he sat beside his wife on their living room couch and casually recalled his feeling about the killing. He said something like, "I remember the next day was Father's Day…I sure felt silly."

Ronald Ebens spoke as if the killing was no big deal, as if it was something that he took lightly. Ronald Ebens's defense lawyer was quick to admit that he himself drove a Japanese car, as if to verify that the crime had nothing to do with either race relations or economics.

Vincent Chin's mother was interviewed, and she discussed how she grew up in Detroit. She said that Chinese immigrants could not aspire to work in the auto plants, but to service white American autoworkers with laundry cleaning or in restaurants. Asians understood how she was brought up to be quiet, follow along, and act as a slave in a white world. She always worried that her son was fooling himself when he assured her he had been "accepted."

Asians must stand in solidarity, and the masses must bring out the issues more publicly. In the words of Malcolm X, they should do so "by any means necessary" and support victimized Asians if they want to prevent Asians from dying senselessly. Take, for example, a case in Queens, from February 13, 2004. A Chinese-food deliveryman got stomped on, beaten with a hammer, stabbed with a knife, and hit with a bat, and then his body was dumped in a nearby pond. The Chinese delivery person was killed for between forty-six and forty-nine dollars.

There was another article in the *Daily News* from October 21, 2005. Another Chinese-food deliveryman was shot dead by two robbers in the Bronx. Stories like these are endless. There are probably many more cases that are unreported.

These examples show that some people don't think that an Asian life is a human life. Some non-Asians view Asians as less than human; thus, they feel that committing harm upon them with no remorse is OK. And many things contribute to this, such as the media. Therefore, Asian people must unite and be courageous to speak up for victims of such crimes, so these acts are not ignored. Moreover, Asians must make sure those committing the crime are held accountable. Asians should put enormous pressure on the judicial system to be sure those individuals are convicted. Asians cannot be weak or show themselves as weak, because non-Asians will see that weakness, and then Asians end up dead.

If Asians want to stop it, because they don't want the next Asian person to die, they must be more involved when there is violence against Asians. They must come out in billions strong to ensure that those people committing these ruthless acts are exposed and prosecuted by the fullest extent of the law.

Asians must always join together to actively seek and destroy those who denigrate and disrespect Asians. Take, for example, an article from *Newsday*, from Thursday, January 27, 2005:

Tarsha Nicole Jones, better known as Miss Jones, was a radio personality at the station HOT 97 (WQHT 97.1 FM). She mocked the tsunami victims in a controversial song that aired on Jan. 18, 2005. The song included racial slurs against Asians and jokes about floating human bodies and orphaned children. The song was set to the tune of "We Are the World," a hit from 1985 about famine relief, sung by many well-known singers such as Michael Jackson, Bruce Springsteen, and so on.

Luckily, New York City Councilman John Liu and Asian advocacy groups called for the hosts' resignations. At least three advertisers abandoned the station, and Miss Jones and some of the morning team were suspended.

Because some Asians got together to denounce the bigotry of Miss Jones and did something about it, results were achieved. However, it's definitely not enough. All Asians must join together as one to let everyone know that Asians cannot be disrespected without any consequences. Asians must show that they have a voice and a very powerful movement.

The next story was covered by *Newsday*. It was also covered by the *New York Times* in an article by Michelle O'Donnell, published Tuesday, August 15, 2006:

College-aged Asian men were driving home around 2:00 a.m. Suddenly a Toyota pulled alongside the victims' Lexus. The men in the Toyota yelled racial, derogatory insults. A few seconds later, the driver of the Toyota decided to slam into the Lexus. The Asian men stopped at some point to examine their damaged car. But the Toyota came back, and two men again yelled racial slurs and began to punch and kick one of the Asian men. Another Asian man came out of the car to help, and he was attacked as well. One Asian man stated he was punched up to fifty times; his eyes were swollen and black when he spoke to the press.

This is a great example of an Asian minding his or her own business and trouble coming. This incident could have been just like the previous cases in which an Asian individual ends up dead; luckily, it wasn't.

Therefore, Asians have to make the outcome different so that others know not to fuck with Asians. Asians need to fight back and prepare for these moments. If every Asian from now on wakes up in the morning knowing he or she may get beaten just for being Asian, then Asians need to defend themselves. These things happen more often than you think but are not always reported. Asians can no longer live in a world where they are always victims. That is why Asians must change the way they think. They must all become warriors and expect that non-Asians may victimize them at any given time. If an Asian is unprepared, then that Asian runs the risk of being beaten up or killed, as seen in all the previous stories. So choose your option: Do you want to be hurt and killed or let other non-Asians realize that if they fuck with you, they will be the ones who are hurt or killed? The choice is yours.

Asians should not shy away from martial arts because they don't want people to stereotype them. They should embrace martial arts because it will save their lives and is part of their culture. In addition, Asians should seek to embrace other non-Asian defenses, such as boxing, wrestling, and the art of war. Whites don't give up Greek wrestling because they don't want nonwhites to stereotype them; nor do African Americans give up boxing. Non-Asians seek to dominate all sports and seek other sports to conquer as well. Asians must think and do the same. Asians should not let others dictate what they should do. They must do things to benefit themselves. They should now prepare to protect their livelihood more seriously. Asians have to get with the program and equip themselves.

On December 5, 2006, Rosie O'Donnell made an anti-Asian slur when she discussed Danny DeVito's apparently drunken appearance on *The View*. She said the incident was being talked about as far away as China and lapsed into a pseudo-Chinese dialect ("ching-chong, ching-chong").

These celebrities believe that it's OK to make fun of, criticize, and denigrate Asians as they please, because there won't be a backlash. As stated earlier, a new Asian generation must come forth and change that.

The following is based on a story from the *New York Times*, printed on Sunday, January 7, 2007:

"In the late 1980s, administrators appeared to be limiting Asian admissions to top universities, prompting a federal investigation. The result was an apology by the chancellor at the time (Ira Michael Heyman,) and a vow that there would be no cap on Asian enrollment." This is why it's important for Asians to fight against and investigate Asian discrimination and to find justice for all.

For example, Jian Li, a freshman at Yale, has filed a complaint against Princeton. He contends that he was rejected because of race and that admissions standards are higher for Asians. Proposition 209, which forbade government institutions from considering race, among other things, for employment or education, was a great and just thing in California, because why should Asians be denied the best schools and education when they meet the merit requirements?

There is a similar article from the *New York Post*, printed Sunday, November 30, 2014, titled "First Jews, Now Asians." The article describes how Asians were similar to Jews after World War I, when Harvard adopted de facto quotas on Jews. There were concerns that the rising number of Jewish students would "ruin" their schools. An Asian American who ranked number one in a high school class of 460; attended a school in the top 5 percent of US high schools; had perfect

800 scores for his SAT II history and math; and was an AP Scholar, National Scholar, and involved in many other activities was rejected by Harvard. Thus, the Students for Fair Admissions group is suing Harvard. The charge is very direct; they state that Harvard is intentionally discriminating on the basis of race. Harvard actually admitted that they take less qualified applicants from other racial and ethnic groups at the expense of more qualified applicants.

In an article from the *New York Post*, printed Sunday, January 28, 2007, comedienne Sarah Silverman was bold enough to say the word "chink." If she had used the *N* word, would African Americans have let her get away with it? Of course not. She used a derogatory word to offend Asians because Asians usually don't fight back. That is a problem that needs to be fixed; the new Asian generation has to make sure of that.

Another article appearing in the *New York Times* on Sunday, March 4, 2007 was about Asians trying to make it as pop stars but being hindered by their Asian looks. They just don't "fit in," because society doesn't recognize Asians as pop stars, no matter how good they might be at singing. Society already stereotyped Asians with the image of studious geeks and the perception that someone who looks Asian must be a foreigner. This clashes with the coolness and born-in-the-USA authenticity required for American pop stardom. Nonetheless, there are many Asians who either were born in the United States or grew up in America.

Singers from non-Asians regions, such as Europe, Latin America, and elsewhere are able to obtain pop stardom. This is why Asians themselves must start their own fan base and have their own followings first. You need to get an audience to follow you, because if you master the craft of singing or acting, you still need to convince an audience to pay to hear and see you. If you can't break the stereotype, you will not break into the industry, so you need to establish a base for those arts among Asians first.

The writer describes Korean American Mr. Kim, who competed on *American Idol*. He sang ballads on the show and was praised by the judges for his "range" and "tonal quality," but he was among the first four contestants voted off by viewers after the first round. While he was still on the show, Mr. Kim wrote on his MySpace page, "I was told over and over again, by countless label execs, that if it weren't for me being Asian, I would've been signed yesterday."

On a positive note, the same article also discusses a twenty-two-year-old pop singer by the name of Natalise. She is of Burmese and Chinese descent, and her single "Love Goes On" was a local radio hit in 2002. In addition, she has had some of her songs, which she also writes, featured on local commercial radio and MTV shows. She is recording her third album on her own label. Natalise stated something key for Asians to know: "I feel that we're (Asians) on the brink of something huge, and it's just a matter of time and effort." All Asians should share her optimism.

Natalise's manager, Andy Goldmark, said, "Asian Americans have lagged behind, not because of discrimination, but because they have yet to create their own popular music sound, the way African Americans and Latinos have."

Furthermore, he said, "Asian Americans have tended to follow what's going on in the pop world rather than using the Asian Americans' path to invent new things."

Again, this is why Asians must do their own thing and be innovative in music while incorporating sounds from African Americans and Latinos. The same way the world incorporates items of Asian origin, such as martial arts, pasta, gunpowder, and so much more, Asians must incorporate items from the outside and make them their own.

The article goes on to describe other challenges that Asian American artists face: "Asians only make up 4 percent of the country's population; they are too small a market and too fragmented in languages and nationalities to offer a solid springboard for aspiring Asian stars the way other ethnic groups have done," said Oliver Wang, a music journalist who teaches about race and popular culture at California State University in Long Beach. "Similarly, there are limited marketing mechanisms at their disposal."

Mr. Hong of ImaginAsian said, "We [Asian Americans] don't have BET," which caters to African Americans. "We don't have Telemundo to have these artists be taken seriously." Telemundo caters to Latinos. This is why Asians from all around the globe must get together to form a strong alliance for musical artists, such as pop stars, to make the percentage of Asians in the audience much greater. The first Asians to create an Asian "Motown" globally will reap astronomical success and profits. Asians should quickly jump to take that opportunity.

THE NEXT STORY IS FROM THE *DAILY NEWS* OF TUESDAY, MARCH 11, 2008:

A thirteen-year-old Asian boy, Kwok Po Lui, was viciously beaten in December at David Broody School in Bensonhurst. The boy lost 90 percent of his hearing due to the attack. Kwok Po Lui was at a news conference, joined by a councilman, an assemblyman, and the president of the United Chinese Association as well as the Community Improvement Association. This was another case of an Asian being beaten because of prejudice. These are not rare cases; there are many cases of Asians being viciously attacked all over the city, state, country, and various parts of the world, and they are not reported. The reason is simple: Asians are perceived to be easy victims. They are looked at like cockroaches that can be stepped on without any fear of recourse. This is why Asians all over the world must change themselves and change this perception of weakness. The time has come for biblical change, change that will amaze the world in epic proportions.

People are insensitive to Asians in the way they do or say things. Take, for example, this story in the *New York Post*, from Friday, May 9, 2008. The article states how a billionaire boss from Blackstone used an analogy to explain his firm's failed deal to buy a mortgage-lending corporation. He said, "Trying to buy a mortgage bank in the midst of the subprime crisis was the equivalent of being a noodle salesman in Nagasaki when the atom bomb went off. Not a lot of noodles left or even people—and that's what happened to us on this deal." If this were said in reference to the Jewish Holocaust or slavery, he would have been boycotted. Yet because it was said about an Asian country, he felt there would be no repercussion. This has to end with Asian solidarity.

THE NEXT EXAMPLE IS FROM USARISEUP.COM, POSTED ON WEDNESDAY, MAY 6, 2009:
It discusses an article written by an Asian American who grew up in America. The young Asian American male felt that because he assimilated so well in America, non-Asians, particularly white people in America, would accept him as an American, not a foreigner. Little did he know he was in for a rude awakening.

This article describes many Asians as having mixed emotion, because in one way they understood that he was coming from the perspective of Asian Americans and the plight Asians had to deal with growing up in America. However, Asians felt he was condescending in his thought process about Asians as a whole, or maybe he was just plain confused.

The article focused on the *O* word, "oriental." The word is considered derogatory by some Asians because it used to mean that any non-European country was substandard, backward, or not on par with Europe. However, it wasn't the *O* word or definition that was concerning in the article. It was the Asian American's experiences and how he rationalized his unfortunate incident with the word "oriental."

The following is an excerpt from "Thinking Orientals: Migration, Contact, and Exoticism in Modern America," from usariseup.com:

> From the time the Chinese arrived in the mid-nineteenth century, migrants from Asia were considered a threat to white labor and society. Categorized as Orientals, these immigrants were demonized as exotic and non-American.
>
> The term was popularized during European colonization of Asia. Asia's goods, labor, and land were exploited by Europeans who saw the people as inferior... Orient means everything east of Europe. The term is inherently Eurocentric, establishing Europe as the standard and the Orient as the "other."

The story goes as follows: the young Asian American male's father (also an Asian American) was driving, and he noticed an Asian driving too slowly. The father cursed and joked, saying "Damn oriental." He was implying that the other Asian driver must have been a recent immigrant, because the stereotype is that Asian people from abroad can't drive and are considered substandard, backward, or not on par. The Asian American father may have believed that because he grew up in America, he was somehow better than Asians abroad and should not be viewed as a foreigner. Nonetheless, he didn't even know or realize that the other Asian driver could also have been an American. Furthermore, he shouldn't have made the conclusion that Asians that are not Americans can't drive, because the notion that Asians from abroad can't drive is completely false. This is a stereotype that non-Asians have about Asians.

The young Asian American son had experience with the word oriental when he was a student. While he was walking at school, a white American student pushed him forward and told him to get out of the way, saying, "You stupid orientals walk the way you drive." He felt, like many Asian Americans, that he should not be called an oriental, because he grew up in America and was not a foreigner. Somehow he thought that he was accepted as an American. Apparently he thought wrong. The best advice to give Asian Americans that think this way is that they will be discriminated against in America, just like African Americans, Hispanic Americans, Middle Eastern Americans, and various people of color. The individual in this story and other Asian Americans are no exception.

That is why Asians should never think that because they grew up in a certain country, joined a certain club, chose a certain profession, or married into another race they are accepted by that group or any particular people. Some non-Asians will always look at Asians in a derogatory, belittling way. Asians from all over the world should never try to find acceptance from non-Asians, because it is never within Asians' control. Trying to make a non-Asian accept you is like trying to light a room using a faulty light switch that could turn on or off at a moment's notice.

Convincing someone to like you or love you is temporary, depending on how the other person feels about you at that particular moment. Emotion fluctuates. Sometimes people love you, and sometimes they hate you. An individual's personality changes and is very inconsistent. Therefore, Asians should never believe that people will love them all the time. With that knowledge, Asians should just acknowledge that racism and prejudice are forever, and they should do their best to understand them, work with them, and navigate their lifestyle with this reality.

With this wisdom, Asians can now concentrate on what they have to do to be the best they can be instead of wasting valuable time trying to be accepted. Trying to find acceptance is wishful thinking, creates false hope, and is futile. It will only stifle your success, which is your deserving privilege. Instead, Asians should have a "take it or leave it" attitude. If a person likes and respects you, great. If not, to hell with that person. You don't need them. Prejudiced people make their own rules, and they have their own thought process and reasoning. As an Asian, you should never think that you will be "accepted" by the society of non-Asians. No matter how hard you try, it will never happen in this imperfect world. Remember the earlier interview with Vincent Chin's mother, who stated after Chin's murder that she always worried that her son was fooling himself when he assumed he had been accepted.

Asian Americans should not carry a false sense of security, thinking because they grew up in America they will be accepted by non-Asians in America. He will never be accepted and should have that thought with him forever. Asians should always perceive that some non-Asians will denigrate, disrespect, and belittle Asians, because history confirms it.

Therefore, always be prepared for those abuses, and don't be overwhelmed with ignorance when you come across it.

When an Asian American states, "I was born in America" or "I grew up in America," what exactly does that mean? Does it mean Asian Americans are better than Asians abroad, or do they want to convince the world that they are white Americans?

So to advise those Asian Americans who have a dilemma growing up in America: don't become a Twinkie. Be yourself, and make your own way. Live your life without trying so hard to find acceptance by another race or nationality. You will be truly accepted for being you, and you won't have an identity crisis.

THE NEXT EXAMPLE COMES FROM THE *DAILY NEWS* OF MONDAY, JUNE 8, 2009:

A Chinese American woman living in a co-op building in Queens, New York sued the co-op board of Mainstay Cooperative for discrimination. She claimed board members tried to reject her application indirectly at first because she was Asian. As stated in the article, the company "waited months after she applied for an apartment to schedule her interview, and then they stonewalled her mortgage company until she lost her financing offer, according to legal papers."

Based on the information from the *Daily News*, apparently it was interpreted by some Asians that when she raised the money with the help of her employer, which was a real-estate company, the board members decided to take a more decisive, active approach. They told her boss that the woman should move to the Chinese part of town and that he should convince her to leave the building. The boss signed a sworn affidavit stating that board members approached him during a visit. They asked if he was Jewish, which he confirmed. They told him "as a Jew, he should understand" that the Asian woman "should live with her people...in the Chinese area."

This is a great example of prejudice that Asian people should know about. They must accept that knowledge and work with it.

When the case was finally heard in court, the Chinese woman was awarded $225,000. However, according to the newspaper article, the verdict wasn't that it was because of racism. She won because they felt she was picked on for her repairs and construction in her apartment, but other tenants performed such renovations with no problem. Common sense would tell you that this was clearly racism. Asians must know and understand that.

As reported in the *Daily News*, Yu Yao, a twenty-three-year-old, moved to New York just two months before she was snatched off the street on May 15, 2010 and dragged into an alley, raped, and fatally beaten with a pipe. She came to New York, worked at a nail salon, and dreamed of studying to be a lawyer. A few months back, it was reported in the news that there were prowlers targeting Asian women because they were easy victims, perceived to be timid, weak, and defenseless.

History seemed to repeat itself in June 2015. It was reported by the *Daily News* that a man name Tyrelle Shaw targeted Asian women, striking them in their faces with a hard object wrapped in a plastic bag.

According to a *Daily News* article printed on February 21, 2012, Assemblywoman Grace Meng said workers at a Boston Market in Flushing constantly referred to her as "La China" during her visit to the chain restaurant. This is a derogatory name used against Asians. Meng felt very disrespected and confronted the workers after paying for her dinner, but they only shrugged. In the same article, a Texas Chick-fil-A employee dubbed two separate customers "Ching" and "Chong," two more racist, derogatory names used against Asians. Meng stated that the recent spate of racism against Asian Americans needs to end.

On September 29, 2013, all the major news networks and newspapers reported the following incident. A group of motorcyclists swarmed an Asian man's sports utility vehicle in Washington Heights, New York, after he hit a troublemaking motorcyclist, who cut him off, and then ran over several bikers to escape. The motorcyclists broke the driver's side window and pulled him out of the car before stomping on him and beating him.

The Asian man's wife and two-year-old daughter were in the car, and the assailants repeatedly threatened his wife during the attack.

This case may or may not have been racially motivated, but a situation where an enormous number of bikers single out a motorist had never happened to this degree. Some Asians said to me that maybe the non-Asian motorcyclists saw an Asian driver in the SUV and decided to pick on him because Asians are easy prey. This incident and many other cases show Asians as victims.

Asians have to stop becoming victims. Asians should no longer allow the perception that they are soft, easy, and dispensable. Asians must finally stand up and fight like vicious warriors, if challenged, to get that respect. This is why Asians must come together to change these images, if they want to survive and show the world a new Asian generation has been born.

Many of these stories are from New York City. What about other cities in the United States where this might be happening? What about different continents or various countries where this occurs but is not mentioned? This is why all Asians absolutely must do all they can to eliminate the idea that they are weak and easy victims. There must be a major overhaul in the way Asians think and live, and there are various ways to change the way the world perceives Asians.

THE NEXT STORY IS FROM NOVEMBER 20, 2014 AT THE PINK HOUSES IN EAST NEW YORK:

A rookie New York Police Department officer named Peter Liang, an Asian American, discharged a single bullet that struck Akai Gurley, who unfortunately died. Officer Liang and his partner were patrolling one of the most dangerous Brooklyn housing complexes in New York City. As stated by various news reports, Liang was a rookie cop in a pitch-black housing-project stairwell, carrying his gun in his left hand and a flashlight in his right hand. He heard a noise in the dark, and his 9mm accidentally discharged, sending a bullet ricocheting off the wall and into Akai Gurley's chest. Officer Liang was indicted in the fatal shooting and faced criminal charges that could send him to prison for up to fifteen years for the death of Akai Gurley. It was, without a doubt, a terrible tragedy for both Officer Liang and the dead victim and his family.

Yet this story, in the opinion of many Asians, has nothing to do with analyzing who was at fault or who is right or wrong concerning the case of a police officer shooting an innocent man. It has everything to do with the double standard. Many white cops are accused of killing people and never get convicted for it. In the case of Ramarley Graham, an eighteen-year-old African American was shot and killed in the Bronx by a white police officer named Richard Haste, who chased him into his house without a warrant. Graham was unarmed. In the aftermath, a grand jury decided not to indict Officer Haste.

In a second case, Eric Garner, an African American, died when a white New York police officer placed him in a choke hold during an arrest. Ultimately, a Staten Island grand jury declined to bring charges against the white officer. There are many stories of white police officers who are not indicted, and these are cases where it seems the deaths were not accidental, like the Officer Liang situation.

Officer Liang did not go there with the intention of kill-ing someone. He didn't know if his victim would be white, black, Hispanic, or Asian. In addition, he didn't know if his victim would be old, young, male, female, or a child. It was dark in the stairwell. He couldn't see clearly, and anyone could have been visiting someone's home for the first time in the projects. It was unequivocally an unfortunate accident. Nevertheless, the grand jury did not want to protect Officer Liang the same way they protected other officers. Many Asians feel it was because he was Asian. It wasn't important for the grand jury to look after him, for two reasons. The first was that they could satisfy public opinion by showing that the grand jury does convict police officers. The second was that the grand jury believed that Asian lives don't really matter. They believed that there would be no backlash from Asian people, because they are very reserved, quiet, passive, and usually don't make much noise. It's something Asians must realize and accept. Only Asians will look after Asians.

Asian pundits gave their opinions to me concerning the three sample cases above, which all took place in New York City. In the two cases of white officers not being charged for allegedly causing the death of their victims, the officers saw who their victims were and understood the situation. In the Eric Garner case, Mr. Garner stated repeatedly that he couldn't breathe, which everyone saw in the videotape. Many people felt that if the officer had heard Garner's plea, he should have lessened the pressure on Mr. Garner, and then he would still be alive. In the case of Ramarley Graham, when the police officer chased the youngster to his home, maybe the white officer should have called for backup. Maybe he should have requested a warrant before entering the home of Mr. Graham instead of shooting him to death while he was unarmed.

In a fourth case, a young man by the name of Sean Bell was killed by a team of plainclothes and uniformed NYPD officers. During the incident, which involved both white and black officers, the police shot at Sean Bell and his two friends fifty times. Bell was killed, and his friends were severely wounded. And, again, none of the officers were found guilty.

The list goes on within New York City, with the shooting of Amadou Diallo, a case in which all of the NYPD officers were also found not guilty.

Yet in the case of Officer Peter Liang, an Asian officer, he did not see his victim, nor did he lay his hands upon him. Liang unintentionally fired his gun in fear, through darkness, which caused a bullet to ricochet and unfortunately kill an innocent man. But, Asian officer Peter Liang was found guilty. Many Asians felt that if cop is convicted for an accident, then all cops should be convicted for any death, especially when the killing seems more intentional.

Based on every story I heard from Asians, only one reason makes sense—extreme prejudice, a double standard, and bias. The rule seems to be: "Do not convict a white cop or a black cop, but feel free to convict an Asian one." The public officials in the judicial system, who were non-Asians, didn't feel the need to protect an Asian cop, like they did with white and black cops.

People should never believe that just because they make laws, they are correct. Laws are made by imperfect people, not by God. When the grand jury decided to convict an Asian cop but not a white or black cop, it was evidence of judicial prejudice. If the oppressors want to convict you, they will do so, no matter how wrong it may be. Asians have to realize that. It's similar to the Vincent Chin case, in which the jury decided not to convict a white person for killing an innocent Asian man.

X

STORIES FROM ASIANS ABROAD

These stories are from Asians living abroad. This includes students from Asia, Asian visitors and tourists, or Asians abroad blogging or participating in online chats. They also provided data to back up their opinions.

An article from the *Herald International Tribune*, printed October 21, 2002 and written by Tad Daley, briefly discusses the Nuclear Nonproliferation Treaty.

At the heart of the Nonproliferation Treaty is a grand bargain, whereby the nonnuclear weapons states agreed never to acquire nuclear arsenals, in exchange for the nuclear weapons states agreeing eventually to get rid of theirs.

Moreover, the nuclear weapons states—pushed hard by a group of middle powers known as the "New Agenda" countries—recommitted themselves to this goal at the thirty-year Nonproliferation Treaty Review Conference in spring 2000. The conference's final statement, signed and agreed to by Washington, pledged "an unequivocal undertaking by the nuclear weapon states to accomplish the total elimination of their nuclear arsenal."

The article continued by pointing out that during the Bush administration's Nuclear Posture Review, released in 2002, "indicates a clear intent to maintain a colossal nuclear arsenal for time without end. It lays out elaborate plans for designing and developing new generations of nuclear weapons for air, sea, and land deployment in 2020, 2030, and 2040. It does not name a date for any 'unequivocal undertaking' on abolition."

Lastly, the writer stated, "The New Agenda countries expressed their astonishment over the audacity of the Nuclear Posture Review in a joint statement just a few months ago. 'Any presumption of the indefinite possession of nuclear weapons by the nuclear weapon states,' they said, 'is incompatible with the integrity and sustainability of the nuclear nonproliferation regime.'"

So the question is, why should any Asian country listen to any country that has nuclear arsenals, when Asian countries cannot have them? It is total hypocrisy. When a country insists that nuclear weapons are vital to its own security but harmful to the security of others, that country becomes hopelessly lacking in credibility.

Asian countries don't debate with the world over what country is allowed to have nuclear arsenals. After all, a bomb of mass destruction was used only on an Asian country, without regard to human lives; North Korea, China, and other

Asian countries have no history of nuking another country. Therefore, why shouldn't an Asian country be able to have nuclear weapons for its own protection and national security, when other countries, such as the United States, Russia, France, England, and Israel, possess nuclear capability and could use it against an Asian country?

Asian countries are always shunned for developing nuclear capabilities, as China or North Korea have done, but other countries in Europe are never questioned or disputed concerning their possession of nuclear arsenals.

In the book *Plan of Attack*, author Bob Woodward states that during the Bush administration, Donald H Rumsfeld, the secretary of defense, said, "Let me see the Korean War plan." Rumsfeld wanted to know if North Korea had nuclear weapons or not, stating, "It sure as hell would make a giant difference if there was war."

The fact that Asian countries are viewed as places for other countries to invade for their own personal benefits or objectives is another reason why Asian countries need nuclear arsenals to protect themselves. After all, there will be a time when a country maliciously lies about an Asian country, creating a magnificent reason to start war on Asian land. This is similar to what happened with Iraq. America accused them of having weapons of mass destruction and went to war, taking preemptive strikes against Iraq and placing the country in absolute disarray, confusion, and chaos. Therefore, the question should be asked: "Should an Asian country have arms to protect itself or not, because a bomb of mass destruction was only used against an Asian country in the past?" Why is it more sensitive for an Asian country to have a nuclear bomb than a European country? Is it because of prejudice toward Asian people?

A Vietnamese native who stayed with friends in New York for a short time gave me an article from the *Village Voice*, dated September 22–28, 2004. The article was accompanied by a full-blown picture of a dead Vietcong soldier being dragged by an army tank after a battle. He looked as though he were roadkill on the side of the road, like a rat, raccoon, or squirrel being dragged purposely for fun—not as a human being. The Asian individual who provided the article explained to me the atrocities and humiliation the Vietnamese people faced during the war, whether they were North Vietnamese or South Vietnamese. He wanted me to read the article, because he believed that Asians are treated more disrespectfully in war than other races. In World War II, when America fought against Germany, there weren't too many shocking stories about American soldiers abusing locals as they did in Vietnam. Americans fighting in Europe kill their enemies and advance, but when it comes to war against an Asian country, there are barbaric incidents.

The article stated:

> John Kerry is being pilloried for his shocking Senate testimony thirty-four years ago that many US soldiers—not just a few "rogues"—were committing atrocities against the Vietnamese.
>
> US military records that were classified for decades but are now available in the National Archives back Kerry

up and put the lie to his critics. Contrary to what those critics, including the Swift Boat Veterans for Truth, have implied, Kerry was speaking on behalf of many soldiers when he testified before the Senate Foreign Relations Committee on April 22, 1971, and said this:

"They told stories that at times they have personally raped, cut off ears, cut off heads, taped wires from portable telephones to human genitals and turned up the power, cut off limbs, blown up bodies, randomly shot at civilians, razed villages in a fashion reminiscent of Genghis Khan, shot cattle and dogs for fun, poisoned food stocks, and generally ravaged the countryside of South Vietnam, in addition to the normal ravage of war and the normal and very particular ravaging, which is done by the applied bombing power of this country."

The archives have hundreds of files of official US military investigations of such atrocities committed by American soldiers. I've pored over those records—which were classified for decades—for my Columbia University dissertation and, now, this *Voice* article. The exact number of investigated allegations of atrocities is unknown, as is the number of such barbaric incidents that occurred but weren't investigated. Some war crimes, like the Tiger Force atrocities exposed last year by the *Toledo Blade*, have only come to light decades later. Others never will. But there are plentiful records to back up Kerry's 1971 testimony point by point.

This, in addition to the shocking story of the My Lai Massacre on March 16, 1968 of 567 civilians in a Vietnamese village—a barbarism unknown to the American public until late 1969—was not an isolated incident in which rogue troops went berserk but simply one of many US-perpetrated atrocities.

The Vietnamese exchange student whom I interviewed wanted to point out that this was a war between North Vietnamese and South Vietnamese, just like the American Civil War. America had no business going into this war, just to commit hideous crimes. No outside Asian country came to America to take sides with either the North or South during the American Civil War.

THERE WAS A SOMEWHAT RELATED STORY FROM THE NEW YORK PAPER *NEWSDAY*, PRINTED WEDNESDAY, JULY 20, 2005:

General Westmoreland referred to the belief espoused by US leaders that if communism were allowed to take hold in one country, it would spread like falling dominoes across the globe.

Then why didn't the United States fight the former Soviet Union? They were the biggest communist threat at the time, not Vietnam. For example, when you want to stop drugs from ruining your community, you don't truly believe that stopping the small-time drug dealer on the streets is the solution; you have to stop the drug lord who is the ringleader.

The same applies to communism. Don't fight a small third-world country and kill thousands of innocent people just to make an example of ending communism. Go for the big honcho who's the real threat, which was the former Soviet Union. The reason why they used Vietnam as an example was because they thought they could win the war on this small country with no real threat to the security of their country and let the world see it. They simply killed innocent Asians for nothing.

This shows that Asians must obtain real strength and power, so that no one will make an example of them, forcing them to become victims. The moral of the story is that each and every Asian country should become a superpower. Then they will not be small and dispensable, like Vietnam, with non-Asian countries using them for political games at the expense of innocent Asians.

THE FOLLOWING CAME FROM *NEWSDAY*, PRINTED MONDAY, DECEMBER 27, 2004:
The number of bombs used in the Vietnam War for the purpose of cutting off North Vietnamese supply lines was double the number of bombs dropped on Germany in all of World War II. Why was it necessary to use more force in a country that was inferior and small, like Vietnam, compared to the force used in powerful Hitler-led Germany during World War II? The only conclusion is that Asian lives were not as important as white European lives. Similarly, it was OK to use a bomb of mass destruction on an Asian country, like Japan, rather than a European country. There are some non-Asians today with guilt, who may try to rationalize why

Asian countries were targeted for mass destruction, but no reason can really justify it.

THE NEXT STORY IS BASED ON A SPECIAL REPORT FROM *TIME* MAGAZINE, MAY 27, 2005: The article is about Xu Jinglei, a movie director and actress. Her accolades and accomplishments include the Best Director award at the San Sebastian Film Festival in Spain. In the article, she states that she wants to show that Chinese people are just like everyone else. She knows the stereotype very well; Asians are supposed to be conservative and mysterious, from some foreign land, fine-tuning their martial art skills. She seemed irritated by the idea that Asians are only viewed this way. She wants people to realize that Asians are actually real people who play, sing, dance, and have emotions and an actual personality.

Another article from *Time* magazine, appearing in June 27, 2005, was titled "China's New Revolution." The article posed a lot of challenging questions. The first question was, "The People's Republic has embraced the modern world as never before. Is that cause for celebration or anxiety?"

This is a probing question, because what is the writer implying? Is he stating that as China progresses into a more modern, sophisticated country, the world shouldn't celebrate and be happy but instead be more anxious because China may be doing better than other countries and someday may lead the world?

Based on the analysis of the non-Asian writer, it's hard to win this situation. If China stayed poor and was a third-world country, it would be criticized for not being able to handle its own economy, government, and people and for lacking innovation and knowledge to compete with world markets.

On the other hand, if China prospers, as they are now, envious countries would want to hold them down. What is China to do? Stagnate and not improve?

Most Asians believe prospering is better. The hell with what the world thinks—excel like never before. Make an empire so powerful that the world will never look down at you again.

The anxiety lies with the oppressors not wanting Asians to advance. Asian people should always analyze questions brought about by non-Asian writers writing about Asian people and countries, to evaluate if the purpose of the writing is to stifle the people's progress. Asians must always challenge it.

The second question was, "Why is Beijing engaged in a major military buildup?"

This is also a peculiar question. Why not?

For centuries, China's history included foreign humiliation, its territory invaded and dismembered, its people raped and massacred. So why can't China finally find its own sovereignty and protect the country? China's history is very different from the French's (Napoleon), the British's (imperialists), Germany's (Nazis), and America's (the military). For the most part, those countries attacked, invaded, and conquered other countries beyond their neighboring borders. Why didn't the writer focus more on those countries who actually annexed other countries to gain resources and wealth?

Answering the writer's question about why China is building its military is simple. China needs to protect its interests and sovereignty from outsiders, as it improves the country's well-being. This is another example of how non-Asians try to hold down Asians.

Anytime a non-Asian writes about an Asian individual, people, or country, you must always decipher and analyze it to see its true implication. Judge the writing to see if it's truthful or filled with deception and alternative motives. A written story may be a way to denigrate or demonize Asians and may be orchestrated in a way to disrupt the Asian cause.

In the same magazine, there is an article about Kang Lingyi, age twenty-four, who is an Internet executive. He is at the forefront of one of the most powerful movements in China today—nationalism. He said, "America is much too involved in China's internal affairs." He goes on to say, "China does not try to impose its human-rights standards on America."

This is a very powerful statement, because America, which is considered a melting pot of various nationalities, cultures, and religion, is still controlled by white Americans. China doesn't ask why white America discriminates against people of color, who are also Americans, and start a debate on what the resolution should be. Therefore, you can't be a hypocrite and give standards to another country when your own standards are questionable.

Let countries resolve their own issues, and eventually they will sort out any problems by themselves, just like any other country.

An article in *Newsday* from Thursday, August 4, 2005 is about the use of the atom bomb in Japan, both in Hiroshima and Nagasaki. The total casualties were 199,000.

Most Asian countries that were victims of Japan in World War II probably wouldn't disagree with the use of the bomb against Japan. But the fact that the bomb was only used against Asian people, and not a non-Asian country, confirms the idea that Asians are more hated than other races. This should show Asians that non-Asians look at Asians differently, perhaps considering them an expendable, inhuman species.

Asians have to be extremely cautious when reading articles by oppressors, because they start off by writing how much they care about Asians. But as you read carefully between the lines, they really mean the opposite—they really don't care about Asians at all. For example, look at the issue of *Newsday*, from Friday, August 5, 2005, page A46. The article begins by saying, "Dropping A-bombs was within World War II's rules." In the article, the writer begins by challenging how historians view the use of A-bomb, and then he continues to write, with some sympathetic feeling, of the horrors of war and the casualties involved. He then writes, "I can't claim to have worked out the moral calculus of bombing. I remain troubled by the deliberate killing of civilians, whether by the United States or by its enemies. *But I don't think the atom bombing of Japan was a uniquely reprehensible event*" (emphasis added).

So with all the twists and turns in his writing, some Asians perceived it as saying, "Killing Asians and using the atom bomb, the only bomb of mass destruction, was not reprehensible in a country where only Asians live." If the atom bomb were used in a European country, you could be sure this writer, as well as other writers of European descent, would have said the use of the atom bomb was definitely reprehensible, because European (white) people should not experience this devastation. So Asians should always read articles written by non-Asians with caution and keenly analyze the language.

On April 22, 2006, the *New York Post* had a picture of former president George W. Bush tugging at the sleeve of Hu Jintao, the Chinese president, at a White House event, because he was walking the wrong way. The headline was "Wok This Way," referring to the traditional Chinese sauté pan. Some Asian organizations, groups, and individuals said it was definitely a derogatory article and extremely offensive, because it implied the president of China was a cook in a Chinese restaurant. The director of the Asian American Legal Defense and Education Fund said, "It was racist and offensive because it takes the president of China and connects him to the stereotype of a cook in a Chinese restaurant." In addition, the deputy executive director of the San Francisco–based group echoed similar feelings, stating that committee members felt the wording was "insulting" and "perpetuates the stereotype of all Asians as cooks in chop-suey joints."

Strangely, the *New York Post* defended its word choice, noting it was meant to convey humor. This should absolutely alarm Asians to the fact that there are people doing their best to disrespect and destroy Asian rights and privileges, because this newspaper is a national paper that could spread incorrect knowledge and perceptions to others. In contrast, if this newspaper used the same or similar wording about an African president or a Jewish president, there would have been a tremendous uproar. But because it was directed toward a group who usually doesn't make an issue of anything, it was OK to be prejudiced. It is time for Asians to truly wake up.

At the end of articles like this, there is always a twist, similar to putting salt on a wound. The writers tried to prove that they are good people. "'The *Post* has enormous respect for the Asian American community,' said a spokesman for the *Post*, which has also been roiled recently by its gossip-page payola scandal. 'They certainly did not mean to offend anyone,' he said."

The Asian person who gave me this news article stated that the real definition of this comment by the spokesman was "We (non-Asians) want to offend the shit out of you all the time and really hate you, but we will try our best to fool you articulately by saying we love you, so that hopefully you'll believe us, and then later we can disrespect you again."

If the *Post* truly respected Asians, they would have never written the article in the first place and would have had an editor make sure nothing in the article was offensive or in poor taste regarding Asians.

In addition, this is not the only newspaper that has used derogatory language toward Asians. The *Philadelphia Public Record* newspaper used racial slurs in a photo depicting City Councilman Mark Squilla with a group of Asians in Chinatown, referring to some in the photo as "Chinky Winky," "Dinky Doo," and "Me Too." If researched, you will discover there are many, many, many similar stories; therefore, it should not be a surprise that some newspapers are in on it when it comes to racism against Asians. As said before, observe how the game is played.

Asians that are interested in coming to America or Europe are hoping to find a better life, not knowing there are things that they should learn first from Asians who grew up in these countries rather than their original Asian homelands. An article from the *Daily News*, May 16, 2007, describes two women from Indonesia who worked like slaves for five years in America. When one of the women escaped, she stated that she was scalded with hot water, ordered to take thirty showers in a three-hour period, and force-fed twenty-five hot chili peppers. In addition, her upper body was covered with bruises. The other woman was forced to take ten ice-cold baths in a row for punishment. Both women were barred from leaving the house. The owners kept them as "house slaves" for years. So it's important Asians learn from other Asians. Asians need a passport of knowledge, before perceiving the world around them as great and beautiful. If not, you could find yourself force-fed twenty-five hot chili peppers and scalded with hot water.

THE *NEW YORK TIMES* SHARED THE FOLLOWING ON SUNDAY, APRIL 20, 2008:

Zhu Xiaomeng used the Internet to take action. She and her classmates were "channeling anger over anti-China protests during the tumultuous Olympic torch relay into a boycott campaign against French companies, blamed for their country's support of pro-Tibetan agitators…More than 20 million people have signed online petitions saying they plan to stop shopping at the Carrefour chain, Louis Vuitton, and other stores linked to France because of what they see as the country's failure to protect the Olympic torch during its visit to Paris."

In addition, the article says that "protesters gathered in front of a half dozen outlets of the French retailer Carrefour, including a demonstration in the central city of Wuhaun that reportedly drew several thousand people, according to Agence France-Presse."

Furthermore, the article shares that "foreign news outlets here have been swamped by angry phone calls; two music videos circulating on the Internet blast CNN with expletives and lyrics like, 'Don't think that repeating something over and over again means that lies become truth.'"

This article gives a great example of how one person can make a difference in communicating and bringing solidarity to millions of people. Just imagine if more people were to follow her lead; then maybe you would have billions of Asians worldwide in solidarity. If this happens, then the world will listen and can't ignore the Asian cause.

The main purpose is to establish respect for all Asians worldwide. It is not to have all Asians believe in particular political ideas or religions but to have a consensus of treating Asians humanely, with dignity.

An article from the *Wall Street Journal*'s weekend edition, dated April 18–19, 2009, was titled "China—Friend or Foe."

The story at first described China as a country rapidly expanding its military, which might be a "threat" in the future. It went on to explain the substantial amount of money China is spending on its military, which is similar information to that of an article presented earlier. Also discussed was China's acquisition of high-tech weaponry. However, the story twisted upon itself as the writer started to poke fun at China by saying, "Despite China's modernization drive, many weaknesses remain in its armory. Chinese military officers' own assessments of their abilities, contained on professional journals and military media, say that they fall short of their goals of being able to fight and win a high-tech local war."

The writer then said, "By the Pentagon's own estimates, China's limited ability to move and sustain soldiers beyond its borders hasn't improved appreciably since 2000." In addition, it adds, "Critically, China has no experience in modern war-fighting. The nation's last significant conflict was a 1979 border war with Vietnam."

What you learn from this cover story is that China is viewed in two ways. First, it makes China seem like a monster about to devour innocent victims if it gets the power to do so. Secondly, it makes China look like a weak punk who you shouldn't worry about. Therefore, you can't win. Because if you are strong, you look like a bully, and if you're weak, you will be made fun of and picked on. So the moral of the story is to take option one, and obtain as much power as you can take for respect, because it's better than being laughed at as in option two. Asians should be so powerful that others will respect them. This will prevent others from asking, "Who are you?"

The reason for building a military is common sense. When the Europeans came to invade and annexed the land they call America today, they justified the genocide, raping, and forced labor, because the Native Americans were not Christians and therefore were considered evil. The annexation was the same with the Hawaiian Islands.

In a modern-day invasion, George W. Bush rationalized that Saddam Hussein was a threat and contrived a story that Iraq may have weapons of mass destruction. Then he issued a preemptive strike to invade and massacre innocent people in Iraq.

This type of reasoning is why many Asian countries are building their militaries, like China. They don't want other countries to make up their own rationalizations for taking over, annexing, and confiscating the sovereignty of innocent Asian people. It's about protecting one's land and people.

The movie *The Interview* was released on June 20, 2014. The movie is about North Korean leader Kim Jong-un. The oppressors show an Asian leader as evil and joke about his physical looks in the movie; this affects perceptions of other Asian individuals. It's similar to the argument about how placing people of color in movies and films as criminals, murderers, rapists, thieves, and gangsters causes people to associate people of color as criminals, murderers, rapists, thieves, and gangsters.

The same goes with continuing to display an Asian face in a bad light just for laughs. After a while, non-Asians will negatively tease a Chinese, Japanese, Korean, Taiwanese, and so forth as looking similar to the evil leader of North Korea. Again, it's a great technique to create prejudice against Asian people as a whole, using the media without truly realizing the psychological effect it has on the Asian race. As stated before, it's the Pavlov technique in psychology. Nevertheless, imagine Asian people making movies about Hitler and constantly trying to associate ruthless leaders with white people to try to increase prejudice against them. Asians never do that.

XI

BELIEFS MUST CHANGE

The numerous true stories told to me by Asian Americans and Asians abroad, along with the supporting articles, convincingly and unequivocally show that the three categories of Asian haters believe the following about Asians:

It is OK to disrespect Asians; it is OK to wrongfully stereotype Asians; it is OK to discriminate against Asians; it is OK to be prejudiced against Asians; it is OK to write derogatory things about Asians; it is OK to perceive Asians as evil people; it is OK to view Asian women as easy; it is OK to exclude Asians from mainstream society; it is OK to incarcerate Asians with or without due process; it is OK to conquer Asian lands; it is OK to take Asians' resources; it is OK to enslave Asians; it is OK to not acknowledge Asians' contributions; it is OK to view Asians as inhuman; it is OK to attack Asians; it is OK to hurt Asians; it is OK to utilize double standards against Asians; it is OK to kill Asians without negative repercussions or consequences.

Asians who deeply care about Asian concerns want the world to know that they must change the mind-set of these oppressors and their behavior toward Asians. For those wanting a decisive change for the betterment of Asians, a revolution must occur; it is necessary and pivotal in order for Asians to resolve their problems. Asians should not accept the oppressors' abuses as the norm.

If Asians don't do anything to change the unfairness brought upon them by the oppressors, then the oppressors will consider all their wrongdoings against Asians as normal and acceptable. Asians surely don't want that.

The reason for these numerous stories was to acknowledge and confirm Asian mistreatment and to make Asians sick and exhausted of hearing these stories over and over again, prompting Asians to finally do something to prevent this from happening again.

Sharing these factual, documented stories would provide evidence to anyone that these biases against Asians exist and are not isolated. Denial is brutal, and accepting the existence of prejudice is vital for understanding Asian issues. There is one main theme…Asians must change this and have the entire race of billions join the effort.

XII

CHANGING THE TIDE IN THE MIND—WORDS OF WISDOM

Now that we've read, hopefully truly understood the problems of Asians, and looked at the historical facts, we must do whatever it takes to change the false perception of Asians. We must change the tide of unfairness, discrimination, and disrespect. Words of wisdom were shared with me from all the various Asians that I interviewed. They provided me with numerous quotes, comments, and factual data to remind Asians how to think on an everyday basis to strengthen their cause. These statements were designed for Asians to remember and keep in mind in their everyday lives, if they want real change concerning Asian issues.

- Asians must go all out, offensively, to make their voices heard; they cannot afford to take tiny steps forward, only to have those steps wiped away, and then take larger steps backward.

- Once Asians know the problem, or what is perceived to be a problem, then it's time to fix the problem.
- The Asian mind of the past was unprepared, and this resulted in negative, major consequences. That is why it is imperative to change the Asian mind of today to be better prepared for whatever Asians may face in the future.
- If you are an Asian individual that is ignorant about Asian issues, then you are *doomed*. If you are an Asian individual that is aware and knowledgeable about Asian issues and don't do anything about it, then you're still *doomed*. Both concepts are unacceptable.
- There are two options for Asians. You could be strong, a warrior, independent, intelligent, respected, and live with honor. Conversely, you could be weak and a wimp. You could become a pathetic slave, hopelessly dependent, disrespected, and humiliated, and die a fool. Being strong is the best choice for Asians.
- Asians from everywhere must understand how they are viewed differently from non-Asians and, at the same time, understand how non-Asians view Asians as the same in a derogatory way. To explain further, some non-Asians think all Asians from various Asian countries are strange, weird, and hideous.
- Asians should always be observant of their appearance and how they act in front of non-Asians who may perceive them in a derogatory way. For example, some Asians, if their teeth are protruding, shouldn't smile too much in front of non-Asians. It makes them

look stupid and ridiculous, like the Fu Manchu type who smiles, wearing his cultural Asian outfit, his two front teeth sticking out, looking like some fool. Perception is everything. Asians should take care of their appearances.

- Asians traveling to other countries they're unfamiliar with should understand the culture of the land, such as what is right and wrong and what is appropriate and what is not, so as not to be perceived as idiots. For example, some Asians abroad come to the United States and scream at the top of their lungs in their native languages while communicating in restaurants, cafés, and other venues. Locals view them as barbaric and wild, like untamed animals. As stated earlier, perception is everything. All Asians need to educate themselves on the world around them.

- As of now, people of other races are not afraid of Asians; they joke about Asians and belittle them all the time. It is time now for Asians to regroup, get together, and overhaul the way Asians do things and how they are perceived. It is time to show people that they are very wrong about Asians, if they think Asians are weak. It is time for the world to witness that they are very wrong about Asians, if they think Asian people are something to laugh about. So now life begins for Asians as they change their lifestyles for the better. Asians will now do things in their daily lives that will change the way they go about their business in order to advance. This will be for the sheer pleasure of dominating and obtaining notorious power, so that the world will take a deep breath as it watches.

- Predominately non-Asian societies want to make Asians look like fools. Asians never requested to be humiliated, but the oppressors are happy to do so. Some non-Asians believe they can do anything to Asians—disrespect them and everything that goes with that. That is because Asians don't really have a voice or backup to fight back. Things urgently have to change for the Asian people. A new Asian race must be born.

- If you are an Asian employed in a predominately non-Asian workplace and feel people's attitudes toward you are condescending, it is because of many years of conditional prejudice against Asians.

- The ideology of America was such that every American would pursue the privilege of being an American. Asian Americans should not be treated any differently, but they are. Asian Americans, not just white Americans, should also be considered first-class Americans.

- The Asian unity cause should not be used to gather Asians together only to self-destruct when separate Asian groups or entities have misunderstandings among each other. Asian unity should be used to destroy the three categories of oppressors of Asian people, who are the Asian haters.

- Asians should realize that the oppressors fight dirty. The beast attacks from the front, back, side, above, below, and every direction, without rules, to get you off your guard and bring you down. Observe the technique so that you, as an Asian, understand how the battle is fought, and you can figure out how to win the war.

- The most dangerous people are the thinkers of the world. A single big, ugly hoodlum in the street could rob and kill one innocent Asian man delivering a fast-food order, but a thinking Asian could kill thousands of hoodlums…or more. Asians should not be afraid of these people doing harm to Asians. Asians need to fight back.

- Asians should never get to a point where they lower their guards with oppressors. With a blink of an eye, they can be taken over like slaves, the ultimate plan of the oppressors.

- Asians should fight to stop the Asian haters, to defeat the beast, like David and Goliath—not because Asians want to be bullies. Asians will be seen in a new way because of how they think and the things they do that will soon manifest. Whose side is God on-the side of the oppressors or the innocent? God will make sure the innocent win.

- Any Asian who decides to speak badly about other Asians publicly for the benefit of the oppressors should be taught a lesson. They should be reprimanded and punished. For example, Twinkies and coconuts are the most dangerous people for Asians. They are truly the worst traitors. They will kill themselves, along with their Asian families and the entire Asian civilization, just to please their oppressors.

- If Asians let the beast continue its abuse, they get used to it and take pleasure in the beast's barbarity. Asians should not accept victimization as a norm by the oppressors.

- When Asians watch television or movies or listen to music or experience other mediums, they should ask themselves questions. Do any Asians included have a personality? Are there any Asians being included at all, or are Asians being overlooked in those mediums? Asians should then ask themselves if they are wasting their valuable time and money with those non-Asian mediums. It would be foolish and detrimental for an Asian to participate in something that doesn't help the progress of Asians, only to get brainwashed along the way. Twinkies and coconuts are unacceptable as Asian representatives in those various mediums.

- If Asians continue to be placed in American media with personalities like trees and rocks in the background, then they are left with no choice but to make their own media sources. The time has come to ignite Asians for change.

- The oppressors should not be allowed to always make double standards for Asians. Asians should always question the double standard and fight it. Asians have the money, intelligence, and discipline to make their own standards. Therefore, Asians should not lower themselves to a lower standard. Asians should not be like the conquered weak, who are naïve and ignorant.

- Be extra cautious of fake Asians, who use the Asian cause for their own advantage and not for the entire Asian race. You know the ones; they spread false prophecy to gain benefit only for themselves, and they couldn't care less for the cause. They are simply rejects that slipped through the cracks.

- Those Asians who fall for non-Asian vanity or faked facades are similar to Asians who allow a burglar into their homes and befriend a traitor. Seeing what a person really is inside is more important than seeing the fake facade that will later prove false. What Asians should really worry about is what goes on behind closed doors, not the fake outward facade of people that hide the truth.

Temporary personalities are what every Asian should beware of. They are fake and not real. When a non-Asian comes up to you and says hi and has a joyful conversation with you for a short period of time, it doesn't mean he or she is a great person and should be trusted. In fact, some of those non-Asian people you encounter could be the most ruthless people you meet. They may want something from you that you don't know.

A great example is the Native Americans who once ruled the land we now call America. When foreigners greeted the Native Americans, they were nice, respectable, and kind, but when the Native Americans least expected it, their land was taken away from them and most of their people were killed, humiliated, and put on reservations. Asians should beware of temporary personalities from non-Asians.

- Asian actors entering into the entertainment industry should be more than geeks or kung-fu toy figures. Asian actors should demand to play more diverse roles in mainstream media.

- Asians should not be at a point where they say it's too late! Asians should always strive to break into any industry or profession and dominate it.

- No one can change an Asian's success but an Asian. Asians have to stop what they're doing and reevaluate themselves in the world. Asians have to channel their energy into self-improvement, self-empowerment, and self-awareness.

- Asians first must achieve their goal of equality in all facets of society, before talking about peace.

- To make things change, Asians cannot make a tiny change; they must make change on a grand, astronomical scale. Asians must use their global majority population to work for them and create influence worldwide for their benefit.

- Oppressors don't want vital knowledge to be disseminated to Asians. For the beast, even a little bit of justifiable knowledge for the benefit of Asians is detrimental. Knowledge and justice for Asians would affect the livelihood of the oppressors negatively. Similarly, slave owners (oppressors) didn't want slaves to be free, because the oppressors wouldn't have the privilege of utilizing free labor to their advantage or have the ultimate control of people's minds and bodies.

- The time will come when people harass Asians. And the question should be: Will Asians be prepared to protect themselves, their sovereignty, their rights, and their liberty? Will Asians get respect? Thus, Asians should prepare earlier rather than later for what may occur in the future.

- The oppressors want to tell you what you are. The oppressors don't want you, as an Asian, to have an identity. The goal of the oppressors is to take your independence and resources from you, and everything else that goes along with them. Therefore, you, as an Asian, will be at their mercy. In other words, the oppressors want Asians to be dependent on them; they don't want Asians to be independent.

- The three categories of oppressors, as mentioned before, want Asians to feel that oppressors have a life, and Asians don't. Asians must make it known that this is not the case. They must shut it down and unite the movement.

- The days of Asians just accepting or tolerating prejudice must come to an end.

- Asians must think of their sovereignty, whether for their people, lands, or reputations, for equality and justice.

- Conquering Asian land and conquering the Asian mind are very similar. Nevertheless, conquering the mind is much worse. Asians shouldn't allow the oppressors to conquer them—period. If they do, Asians

ARMSTRONG MILLAMENA

will lose their culture, their dignity, their identity, and everything else.

- The oppressors consider it controversial to allow Asians the right to speak, think, and opinionate, because in their eyes, Asians are slaves.

- In the eyes of the oppressors, being American has nothing to do with being born or raised as an American with American citizenship; it has everything to do with Asians following what the oppressors want them to do and complying with their version of being American. The oppressors want to implement their vision of what an American is, not what an Asian American thinks an American is. America was built by a melting pot of people from all over the world, including people of color, and this made America very rich and prosperous. But the oppressors think differently and have their own version of what an American should be.

- America is not a nationality, like a single race of people. It is a system, a way of life, and a country that was conquered and quintessentially made up—it is a melting pot. Nevertheless, the oppressors' view is that Asians, because of the color of their skin or slant of their eyes, should not be accepted as Americans. This is despite the fact that these Asians were either born or raised in America, the same way other immigrants arrived in America, which was originally inhabited by Native Americans.

- If you understand America, you understand that African Americans and people of color from various ethnicities don't follow white America in the white European view of what is American. Instead, people of color live their lives how they want to live them in America, catering to their culture, through music, food, and so forth. So why should Asian Americans follow white Americans to be accepted in diverse America?

- Asians should not yearn for acceptance from non-Asian individuals. Instead, understand racism, acknowledge it, work with it, and maneuver it. Asians should not do everything they can to try to be accepted by non-Asians. If non-Asians don't accept Asians, then Asians should not care about what they think. Asians must have a "take it or leave it" attitude. Asians must do whatever they can to make their own way and accept their way instead of always trying to please others who don't want to be pleased, regardless. Asians should not compromise themselves to please the Asian haters. One can never please another, if one is never pleased to begin with.

- Asians should not be fooled by all the hype—it's like going to a nightclub or party and seeing all the celebrating. You dance and feel like you're part of the oppressors' crowd, but then the crowd turns against you. Or you drink and enjoy yourself with the oppressors, and then suddenly they slip a pill in your drink to get you sleepy or drunk, and when you least expect it, you get raped. Watch out when the oppressors try to make you feel accepted.

- Asians will never be fully accepted in the society of some non-Asians. For non-Asians to accept you a little more, you need to be out there and be seen and show that you have a pleasing personality. For example, Jeremy Lin from the NBA is one Asian individual who has exposure and shows that he has an acceptable personality.

- It's the plan of the oppressors to tell twisted lies to all Asians, so that Asians get fooled and let their guards down, and the oppressors have power over Asians. Oppressors do their best to destabilize Asian unity.

- Here is a thought for all Asians: do something about Asian issues and change your ways, or do nothing and get killed with wishful thinking that something might change.

- The less informed you are as an Asian, the more others will take advantage of you. Being uninformed should not be an option for Asians. The oppressors would like to divide Asians so that they become enemies among themselves, and unify Twinkies and coconuts.

- Asians cannot afford to ignore the past. Asians must learn from the past and realize that the weak were conquered and humiliated. This should no longer be accepted. The new Asian generation must know this and become victorious. They should become so intelligent and physically superior that it shocks and stupefies the mind of the brightest of men. Asians will redefine the meaning of "survival of the fittest." Moreover, it must be done diligently, with extreme discipline and know-how.

- Asian causes must be looked at as a wake-up call, like a category-five storm, a tsunami, or a holocaust coming our way. Asians must awaken with a sense of urgency, or they will be unprepared for the extreme devastation of Asian genocide committed by the oppressors.

- If Asians were to use pity or extreme kindness to win the hearts of non-Asians, it would be a terrible mistake, because you can't please the oppressors. Oppressors view kindness as a weakness.

- Only strength and self-empowerment will get respect for Asians. Extreme power equals extreme respect.

- Asians must use the same tactics that the three categories of oppressors use. If non-Asians are rude and nonnegotiable toward Asians, then Asians also have to be rude and nonnegotiable toward non-Asians. "An eye for an eye; a tooth for a tooth."

- Oppressors don't want to listen to Asians making sense. Oppressors find it easier if Asians are viewed as nonhumans. The oppressors do this so they can trample Asians, just like roaches, without feeling any remorse.

Asians must know this, and they must provoke a revolution in the mind. Given, some non-Asians think Asians are not real human beings; they think Asians do not have real lives and are not real people. They think they can do anything to Asians. In fact, they think they can even kill an Asian without having any negative consequences or backlash, because in the oppressors' minds, Asians are not real, living people. The oppressors could not be prosperous if they viewed Asians as real people. It is similar to the concept of slavery, when it was more prosperous and rewarding to have people working like animals than to have them treated as actual human beings. Making Asians inhuman benefits the oppressors. It is vital and urgent for Asians to come out in full force to get the word out before the entire Asian race becomes slaves and servants in a cult.

- Asians should not be accustomed to slavery, whether physical or mental. In the book *Narrative of the Life of Frederick Douglass*, he writes, "I had somehow imbibed the opinion that in the absence of slaves, there could be no wealth, and very little refinement."

- Asians should always prepare for the worst, as the beast is always planning to incarcerate Asians for its purposes.

- Asians must learn how some non-Asians think when they are in elementary school, junior high school, high school, and college, because it is during those early years that many non-Asians show their true prejudice against Asians. However, once some of those non-Asians mature, or graduate from school institutions or trade school, and begin their careers in the workplace, they are able to hide their prejudice in the real world. Nevertheless, keep in mind some non-Asians already developed their prejudice in their younger years. Therefore, an Asian could meet a non-Asian lawyer, judge, public official, or police officer and think that just because the person has a profession and title that person is supposed to be of a higher standard and free from prejudice—but don't believe it. Sometimes a person who is prejudiced as a child will grow up and still be prejudiced as an adult, no matter what uniform, profession, or title he or she may obtain.

- Once Asian people realize how everything is interrelated, they can begin to understand how their livelihood, economic vitalization, and financial stability are intertwined with race and factors dealing with race. Then Asians will begin to understand how everything works and prosper with that knowledge. Asians must understand how the world looks at them. It's imperative for every living Asian to understand and be exposed to the knowledge, see the way the world operates, and open their eyes, which will let them change their ways forever for the better.

- Asians who didn't grow up in America should be knowledgeable of how they are viewed as well as how they differ from Asian Americans, regarding their upbringing and situation. This will allow them to come to a mutual understanding of each other and how they are viewed by the world with different perspectives.

- Asians should not wait for a tragedy like the murder of Vincent Chin to happen again before they prepare for security or self-preservation. They should prepare now. Prejudice will be stronger than ever, as oppressors take to their campaign more vigorously. Prejudice is alive and well, and Asians should not treat it lightly. The question is, if you don't prepare to protect yourself, are you ready to be an innocent victim?

- The mainstream media is not there to tell the truth but to sway you and categorically fool you into thinking their way. All Asians should be aware of that.

- If Asians love watching various well-known sports that don't include Asians, they must do their very best to break into these numerous sports and dominate them. Asians must support and fund the new generation of Asians, so that they can succeed, compete, and prosper in these various non-Asian sports.

- You can't stop a person from becoming a repeat offender, whether the person is a thief, child molester, alcoholic, or drug addict; therefore, you can't stop a person who was once a racist from becoming a racist again. A person's personality changes at a moment's notice, especially when certain things happen. When and if the atmosphere changes concerning Asians, non-Asians will unite to discriminate against Asians again. For example, during World War II, the people in the United States became racist against all Japanese, whether Japanese Americans or Japanese in Japan. Thus, every non-Asian who used to work with Japanese people before World War II joined together to hate Japanese people and display prejudice toward them. In addition, the prejudice carried over to all Asian people, even those who were not Japanese.

- Asians should realize and fully understand that the non-Asian media has a way to sway people's perceptions and viewpoints. The media is a gargantuan psychological resource that can easily manipulate and sway the minds of the gullible. This is why Asians must have more influence in the media—to change the portrayal of Asians. Asians should not expect non-Asians to change the negative portrayals of Asians. Only Asians can do that.

- When Asian activists write or speak about Asian issues, be careful of non-Asians taking what they say out of context. Many times non-Asians pick and choose from what Asians write and say, then try their best to take things out of context to negate, disregard, and tear down the message that the Asian activists are trying to convey.

- When Asians hear a non-Asian talk or write about Asian issues or concerns, they should listen to or read what is said carefully. They should consider the implications and decide if the ultimate intent of the non-Asian writer or commentator is to provide subliminal messages for the destruction of Asians as a whole. No non-Asian should write about Asians and say who or what they are. Asians should not let anyone else write their history.

- When non-Asians write about Asia's political affairs, be cautious, because many times it's to instigate quarrels and fighting among Asian countries. Outsiders are jubilant for the greater outlook—chaos within Asian communities. This entices outsiders to come in and benefit from Asia's destruction.

- Oppressors think in a different way than ordinary, peace-loving Asian people. Oppressors will always rationalize that they are doing the right thing by doing something wrong and then make excuses when they realize they are wrong. However, they will enslave and humiliate you along the way.

- Asians don't know it yet, or maybe they do, but they have a tremendous advantage over other races when it comes to discipline and achieving success. They have the tenacity to be determined and focused, qualities to accomplish their objectives and goals.

- Some non-Asians are raised and cultured in a way similar to wild animals; they think Asians are prey, ready to be devoured as game, because modern Asians are perceived to be meek, weak, and nonthreatening. This creates the potential for innocent Asians to have their hard work and effort taken away from them, harmed and ruined by the wild beast (oppressors). The wild animals need to be controlled in the way a skilled hunter captures and tames the ruthless, wild beast. Therefore, Asians must become equipped hunters.

- Asians are disrespected by the media and shown as unlikable; thus, it's easy to have them hated and discriminated against. Asians should be aware of that and change the habits of other non-Asian people by being out there with more exposure and involvement.

- Asians should always accept prejudice as a reality and work with it. Asians should not look at things as fine and dandy and go through life thinking there are no Asian issues. Sweeping it under the rug doesn't clean up the problem or fix it.

- Asians countries should be able to possess nuclear arsenals to protect themselves from other non-Asian countries. It's hypocritical for other countries to do so while criticizing Asian countries for trying to acquire nuclear arms for their own sovereignty. Double standards should not exist regarding critical Asian issues and concerns.

- Due to a high international population, Asians have a lot more influence and buying power than people think. Asians have to understand the law of proportion (how many people are within the Asian society). There are *billions* of Asians worldwide, and that cannot be overlooked. If Asians worked together, they would be an overwhelming force to be reckoned with. When you have billions of people united as one, you can be sure that's real power.

- Asians should not be smoke screened by not seeing the clearer picture. The medium outlets may make it seem that the Oppressors are bigger than life, and are the majority, but in actuality, they are the minority. Since Asians are the world's majority, if they also think as one, they could be a biblical force to create change, and influence.

- Asians should look in the mirror and finally come to terms with themselves to accept and realize whether they truly know what's going on around them. Asians must do their very best to change what's going on around them. Asians must no longer conceal their feelings and just accept whatever happens around them; they have to do something to make a change for the better.

- Non-Asians as well as gullible Asians use buffers to fool Asians. A buffer is a made-up *mediator/negotiator* giving Asians a false sense of security. The definition of a buffer is any individual that makes Asians think and feel the world is a better place if they get along with the oppressors. Buffers want Asians to think everything is equal and fine, but it's not. Asians should never believe buffers.

- No non-Asian should have the power to dictate what Asians should or should not do with their lives.

- For Asians, if the oppressors build a wall to shut you out, then break through it. If they close the door in front of you, then find another one to open. Any obst acles the oppressors place against Asians should be brilliantly sidestepped while Asians keep their eyes on the prize.

- If Asians don't speak out, it will be a sign of absolute weakness. If other non-Asians choose to polarize Asians, then Asians must do the same. Funneling money out of Asian resources to things that don't include Asian participation is clearly dumb, because Asians are the global majority. If America or a European country that has diverse nationalities truly wants to be known as a melting pot that respects everyone, then Asians must be respected and included in mainstream society. If not, Asians should not deal with or work with them.

- Asians must persuade others to implement mandatory Asian studies worldwide, to educate non-Asians so others are more familiar with Asians in general.

- The oppressors love to play the role of a judge handing down sentences to the suppressed or oppressed and having control, whether they are right or wrong. Even if the oppressors are wrong, they like giving out unjust sentences, showing they are in control and have the power. Oppressors want to feel important, pointing their fingers at Asians and telling them what they should do and follow, like a dictator to a peasant. Asians should not let them have that privilege. Asians must observe this and fight it.

- Oppressors use power to behave unjustly toward Asians. Asians should not allow oppressors to become judges, like those in court, with power to give a definite answer that affects Asians in a negative way. Asians should keep close watch on their everyday activities to observe the injustices Asians may face or be subjected to and do their best to acknowledge and defeat it.

- Asians must comprehend the difference between reading print and watching television or movies. It takes no effort to watch television or movies, as opposed to picking up a book or newspaper and reading it. Asians must read real nonfiction, important things to educate themselves—not what's conjured and made up in films, which could be exaggerated and manipulated. Keeping Asians uneducated is the tool of enslaving one's mind. Oppressors are able to take advantage of Asians who are not educated. Thus, Asians must make it their duty and diligence to know about Asian issues, so that they will not be taken advantage of.

- The truth will never be uncovered if you hide it with a blanket of concealed, contrived lies. The beast is extremely talented at hiding the truth.
- Silence will be the tool that pierces the heart so that it beats no more. If Asian Americans and Asians abroad expect to survive, they must speak out and be heard across the globe.
- Part of propaganda is making things up, which the oppressors do all the time. They would find a magnificent reason to start war on Asian land.
- The reason why oppressors laughed at Asians and disrespected them was because Asians allowed them to do that. The reason why the oppressors became rich and some Asians became poor was because some Asians foolishly gave them the money without realizing it.
- Oppressors are happy when you fear them, because it gives them strength. That is how they get stronger.
- Conquerors like to reinvent the meaning of many things, because they took control and ownership of your possessions; this helps the beast. It's up to you whether you want to believe the redefining of the meaning and fall prey to mental captivity and lower self-esteem, held down and oppressed thereafter.
- Asians must understand who the enemies are! Anyone holding Asians down from progressing is an enemy. Hidden hatred is lurking inside some non-Asians and needs to be realized, confirmed, and accepted by the Asian communities. Asians who fail to accept the fact that people are prejudiced against them are in serious

denial, and this could be very detrimental to them in the future.

- One of the main objectives for Asians is to let the world know Asians are different from the numerous countries they're from, and stereotyping them as all the same is a great mistake. Asians worldwide must define themselves apart from where they're from and how they grew up. Non-Asians should not do the duty of defining what an Asian is.

- Asians should be giving a heads-up to other Asians about any upcoming, urgent issues, in order to protect them. Asians cannot let injustice be hidden, because if they do, the injustice may happen to them.

- Asians have to start thinking differently; their mindset must change. What went wrong for Asians is that they did not think about what other people were thinking and planning. Then, without notice, Asian people were taken over, losing property, liberty, justice, and so much more.

- White European people should not be looked up to, like Superman in the comic books or white knights in shining armor or heroes landing on Earth to be the protectors of Asians. People of color from various ethnicities don't fall for that trick and trap; why should Asians?

- Asians have to bring back the Genghis Khan spirit and the spirit of previous dynasties in China, when they were warriors and conquerors. Asians should not back out during a fight; they should always train to defeat the Asian haters. If Asians believe they have to come back another time to win, then so be it. Asians will come back to win a battle viciously, like a ninja awaiting his foe. The Asian dragon must awaken to do its deed.

- Once Asians acknowledge and accept how the world views them, then they can move on. Then Asians could try to annihilate the oppressors' mind-sets, before the oppressors annihilate Asians. Asians must watch carefully how they are portrayed in the grand scheme of things, address it, and then do whatever it takes to conquer it.

- James Brown, a legendary African American singer, sang in one of his songs, "I'm black, and I'm proud." Asians must feel the same way about their own ethnicity.

- Asian Americans should strive to be like former New York City councilman and former New York City comptroller John Liu, a Democrat. He is an Asian American who is a great example of an individual who helps his people as well as the community.

- A new generation of Asians must unite as one in solidarity concerning Asian causes.

- Asian haters committed all these crimes against Asians in the past because Asians didn't do anything to fight back; now it's time for Asians to rise, finally fight back, and show the world they're not cowards. Imagine billions of Asians from diverse backgrounds, standing strong and thinking as one, getting together and ready to give the ultimate beat down, if challenged; this is something Asians have not done yet.

- A revolution should happen now. A new generation of Asians should be formed because of the humiliation from the oppressors since the beginning of time.
- There will be anger and hatred displayed by Asians due to the oppressors' biased acts. This will galvanize Asians in such a way that the world of non-Asians will cry for mercy for their wrongdoings. Asians should no longer be embarrassed about themselves, because others made that happen. Oppressors could indirectly commit genocide on Asians without them knowing anything about it. Anger within the souls of Asians should fuel them to achieve justice and real equality. In turn, Asians would gain the respect they deserve. Anger could lead to strength. Let Asians' justifiable anger and intensity help them to emerge victorious.
- Asians could literally change the world if they were all on the same page. Once they decide to change, an enormous metamorphosis would take place for the benefit of all, whether Asian or not.
- Asians should not be disrespected like slaves. Each and every Asian should stop thinking like a slave and think as a master. No longer should an Asian think like a follower but like a leader—a righteous conqueror.
- Asians should not be afraid to offend if it means bringing the message to people. Asian issues are bigger than that.

- If Asians don't do anything to manifest themselves to the world, then the world will choose to view them however it feels like viewing them.
- If you are an Asian who wants change, then you deserve everything. But if you are an Asian who avoids the truth and does nothing, then you deserve nothing. Asians should always understand how non-Asians perceive them.

Now that Asians have shared some words of wisdom and figured out what to do to change the tide against them, they should also champion and recognize those Asian individuals that helped gradually pushed the tide the other way. Even though Asians have had a lot of disparaging setbacks, the tide is slowly shifting. If Asians continue and focus, things will get better. The following chapter will discuss Asians who broke the stereotypes and made changes for the betterment of Asians.

XIII

CHANGE HAS COME: THE ASIAN ACCOMPLISHMENT

Changing the stereotypes means Asians have to be more involved globally, venturing into other careers and industries that they are not known for. For example, participating in such things as sports and entertainment and gaining more mainstream exposure would help the Asian cause. Instead of watching sports or other entertainment, they should become the athletes and entertainers. You should not worship non-Asian athletes or entertainers, because if you worship non-Asian athletes, you become complacent and never aspire to be like them.

THE FOLLOWING ARE EXAMPLES OF PROGRESS AND CHANGE FOR ASIANS:

Asians can compete. Even when the odds are against them, they can come from behind to win. Y. E. Yang from South Korea won the PGA Championship on August 16, 2009. He wasn't supposed to win, because Yang was ranked 108th in the world at the time, and he is Asian. However, he persevered and became the first Asian to win a men's major, against half-Asian Tiger Woods. This is what it means for Asians to challenge themselves and break new ground in society; they abolish the stereotypes that Asians can't do this or that. It is God's will that the oppressors see the world in a different light when it comes to oppressing a certain group of people.

One way of creating change and progressing is including Asians within the world we know. For example, Asian athletes should enter the arena in the world's spotlight. Look at athletes such as Yao Min, who formerly played basketball for the Houston Rockets; former Yankee baseball player Hideki Matsui, better known as "Godzilla"; Daisuke Matsuzaka, pitcher for the Boston Red Sox; and Manny Pacquiao, numerous world title winner in boxing. These are only a few Asians who have decided to take the spotlight and show the world that Asians can enter sports and dominate as well. We need more Asians to challenge themselves a lot more. A vast tidal wave of Asians need to enter various arenas of the world, not only in sports but in every career or profession out there that is not known for having Asians. They need to dominate them to prove to the world that Asians can do anything. To change perceptions, Asians have to be out there and take it and let everyone watch, so eventually people will no longer believe the stereotype about Asians. The past culture of Asians being extremely polite in competition must be thrown out with the garbage, because modesty has no real place in winning.

In June 2011, China's Li Na became the first Asian player to win a Grand Slam singles title, winning against defending champion Francesca Schiavone in the French Open finals. And let's not forget Asian American Michael Chang's 1989 French Open Grand Slam win over Ivan Lendl, the world's number-one reigning Australian Open champion and the three-time former French Open champion.

Michelle Kwan, an Asian American, earned the designation of most-decorated US figure skater, with an unprecedented forty-three championships, including five world championships (1996, 1998, 2000, 2001, 2008); eight consecutive and nine overall US championship titles (1996, 1998–2005); and two Olympic medals (silver in 1998, bronze in 2002). In her career she has received fifty-seven perfect 6.0 marks in major competition, more than any other single skater.

As stated previously, Hideki Matsui, Yao Ming, Michael Chang, Manny Pacquiao, and Jeremy Lin are great examples for Asian males, because they break the stereotypes. They are Asian males who can play a sport usually not known for Asian men. They are the entrepreneurs for the Asian race. We need many, many more of them.

When observing the Olympics, you see many Asians from various countries showcasing their physical talents and winning countless Olympic medals, in categories such as gymnastics, swimming, and other various competitions. This shows that Asians are able to compete physically.

It is not only sports that Asians should delve into; Asians should explore more diversified fields and industries.

Leroy Chiao was a first-generation Asian American astronaut. He was part of the 1994 *Columbia* shuttle. After Leroy Chiao had a couple more successful shuttle missions, he proved himself as a distinguished, competent astronaut. NASA gave him the opportunity to fly with Russian cosmonauts and command a six-month mission on the International Space Station in 2004. He then voyaged to a five-hour spacewalk outside the International Space Station on January 26, 2005. He is another Asian American who defied stereotypes of Asians as Laundromat and restaurant owners. There is nothing wrong with owning Laundromats and restaurants, but it's important for Asians to diversify so that non-Asians know they can do it all.

Detective Agnes Chan became the NYPD's first Asian female officer. She was committed to building bridges between the Asian community and the police department. A native of Hong Kong and raised in New York, she graduated at the top of her police academy class. Promoted to detective in 1984, Chan served twenty years in the NYPD, including time in Chinatown's Fifth Precinct. She retired in 2000.

Ti-Hua Chang is a prominent television journalist based in New York City. With his independent mind, Chang ignored his journalist father's advice to become a doctor and decided to seek out his own career. It paid off, because Chang has been awarded the Peabody, Edward R. Murrow, and numerous Emmy Awards for his investigative journalism. One of Chang's great accomplishments was being able to discover the four witnesses to the murder of Medgar Evers in 1963.

In 2001, John Liu became the first Asian American elected to legislative office in New York history, representing District

Two, in northeast Queens, as a New York City councilman. John believed early on that great leadership and being a visionary, along with hard work, could create a rock solid community. John Liu was also elected as comptroller for New York City. His story is similar to that of many immigrants— one full of determination and a desire to succeed.

Jerry Yang cocreated the Yahoo! Internet navigational guide in April 1994 with David Filo and a year later cofounded Yahoo! Inc. It has since become one of the most trafficked networks on the Internet.

In 2005, Steven Chen cofounded the video-sharing website YouTube, with coworkers Chad Hurley and Jawed Karim.

Sometime before 1865, "Poison Jim," a squirrel trapper, discovered the mustard plant. Highly valued in China and Europe, it was growing like a weed in the Salinas Valley. California's grain growers hired him to remove the "nuisance," and Jim sold the seeds to a French buyer for a high profit, unintentionally turning mustard into a commercial crop.

In 1888, Lue Gim Gong developed an orange that was both sweet and frost resistant in Deland, Florida. The "valencia orange" earned him the Silver Wilder Medal from the American Pomological Society in 1911.

In 1909, inventor and aviator Fung Joe Guey made the first successful flight of a heavier-than-air, motor-driven airplane on the West Coast when he flew a big biplane a half mile above a grassy knoll at Piedmont Heights. His story later inspired author Lawrence Yip to write the book *Dragon Wings*.

Remarkably, the first Chinese American to earn a US pilot's license was Tom Gunn. Starbulletin.com explains that Mr. Gunn actually represented China in the 1910 International Aviation Meet in Los Angeles. Gunn was considered and dubbed the "Wright of China." He was contacted by Sun Yat-Sen to popularize aviation during 1911. In a period of two years, Gunn impressively made more than eight hundred flights and carried more than three hundred passengers in the Pacific region, including the Havana Islands, where he also demonstrated the first flying boat.

Chien-Shiung Wu came to the United States to study science as a teenager and became the world's foremost female experimental physicist. Wu received the National Science Medal in 1975 and the Wolf Prize in 1978 for her significant contributions to nuclear physics. To many scientists she is known by the nicknames "First Lady of Physics" and "Madame Curie of China."

Steven Chu enabled a quantum leap in the study of the relationship between matter and energy by devising a brilliant method for using six lasers to trap and cool sodium atoms down to 240 millionths of a degree above absolute zero. His work won him the 1997 Nobel Prize in physics. In 2009 President Barack Obama appointed him the US energy secretary.

There are endless examples and stories of Asians accomplishing in a diverse array of fields, which could go on and on into eternity, but the main point is that no oppressor of Asians can stereotype Asians as doing only one thing.

If Asians begin to consciously and aggressively dominate and saturate all markets in various fields, professions, and industries, then non-Asians would no longer be able to stereotype Asians as just doing one thing, and that is the absolute goal for Asians.

XIV

Personal Opinion

As I was writing this book and soaking in a tsunami of information from various Asian individuals and groups, I couldn't help but give my own limited personal opinion. To some Asians who were angry about the wrongs committed by non-Asians, I presented an article written by Jenny Deam. The article is from the June 20–26, 2008 issue of *Rise Up* and can also be read at usariseup.com. I decided to provide this article because I felt there are many non-Asian individuals who also help the Asian cause.

The story was about a great man named Ralph Carr. He was the governor of Colorado during the time when Japan bombed Pearl Harbor. It was during this time that anti-Japanese sentiments escalated all across America. It didn't matter if you were from Japan or a Japanese American who grew up in the United States; if you were of Japanese descent, you were the enemy. However, Ralph Carr didn't feel that way. He did not agree with what the rest of America was thinking. Japanese families left their homes in Los Angeles, traveling by cars and pickups. They avoided illegal capture by the US government, which would have brought them to live in barbed-wire camps. When they entered Governor Ralph Carr's state of Colorado, they were greeted by a trooper who said, "Governor Carr and the people of Colorado welcome you."

Ralph Carr said, "If we imprison American citizens without evidence or trial, what's to say six months from now we wouldn't follow them into that same prison?"

In addition, the article states, "It infuriated him that citizens could have their rights so trampled by their own government."

Carr once declared that the US Constitution begins with "We the people…" He said it doesn't begin with "We the people who are descendants of the English or the Scandinavians or the French." Ralph Carr, the Colorado governor, sacrificed his own rising political career and died denounced and forgotten because he defended the rights of Japanese Americans.

I presented this story to show that there are some non-Asians that are great to the Asian people, because some of the stories I was hearing made most non-Asians sound as though they were predators.

Asians reminded me that they were not disputing the fact that some non-Asians are outstanding and magnificent individuals who do not hold prejudice toward Asian people. But at the same time, those great non-Asian individuals are only a tiny proportion with limited powers. Therefore, those good non-Asians, for the most part, cannot help the entire Asian movement; only Asians can do that.

Some Asians also pointed out that the same article describes the situation in Wyoming, the neighboring state to Colorado. There the governor promised, "A Jap hanging from every tree." In Kansas, the governor vowed to call out the National Guard to keep Japanese Americans out of his state. Within Colorado, a front-page headline in the *Denver Post* called the Japanese "yellow devils." Some called for Carr's impeachment. In addition, President Franklin Roosevelt authorized the removal of tens of thousands of Japanese Americans from their homes and businesses on the West Coast, because they were viewed as a possible threat during wartime.

The article I presented was counterproductive, because they argued that for every non-Asian that backs up Asians, there are many more that don't. Furthermore, the non-Asians that back up Asians are not the ones holding the ultimate power or the people that could make real change for Asians. Again, I was reminded that only Asians could change the situation for the better.

My interviewees made an analogy to current times: when Asians are friends with non-Asians, those non-Asians usually don't have major influence to make policies that would assist or help Asians in crisis. The example they gave was the infamous story of Vincent Chin. When Vincent Chin went to celebrate his bachelor party with his white friends, they just watched and didn't help while two white murderers killed Chin with a baseball bat.

On a grander scale, during World War II, Governor Carr wanted to stop the illegal detention of Japanese Americans.

But his hands were tied, because the people in power, such as President Roosevelt and other governors, overruled his decision. Thus, this idea applies to modern days. When an Asian has many non-Asian friends, those non-Asian friends do not necessarily have the political pull or power to really help make improvements for Asians. In a nutshell, those non-Asian acquaintances are not capable of combating the majority of racist oppressors who make the rules and policies.

I found myself quarrelling, debating, and going back and forth a tremendous amount with some Asians on various topics and issues. I also gave them my own life story: that I grew up in America, in a predominately Italian American neighborhood, with a vast array of people of color everywhere in public schools. I saw my share of prejudice, but not to the point that I became prejudiced myself. For the most part, I assimilated very well with all races, whether black, white, Latino/Hispanic, or others. People from various nationalities liked my company, and my relationships were mutual.

I was a very athletic individual. As an Asian child, I did more push-ups and sit-ups in a minute than anyone in the entire school, regardless of race. In fact, during grade school, my gym teacher wanted to put me on the popular TV show *That's Incredible* to showcase my physical ability. In junior high school, I received a trophy at graduation for being the number-one marathon runner in my school. My physical talent continued during college, where I was a champion in martial arts. Everyone knew me for my physical talent, and I did break stereotypes of Asians being nerds and not athletes.

I was very outgoing and played a lot of sports and hung out with everyone from various races, religions, and nationalities.

I didn't have the gruesome experiences that Asians I interviewed had or witnessed. Nevertheless, as I spoke, Asian students and others reminded me that my circumstance and situation were different and could be considered exceptional. Furthermore, Asian issues aren't about one person or group; they're bigger than that; it's about an entire race as a whole, with a history that dates back centuries. I was advised that if I'm serious in writing about Asian issues, the writing has to be based on the great majority, not a single person.

I was accused of being a buffer and holding Asians' hands back as they tried to fight the enemy oppressors. Therefore, I decided to shut up and listen. However, I asked one simple and straightforward question. I was annoyed with hearing the limitless, pathetic Asian stories that made it seem like Asians always fall prey to the beast without a fight. I boldly asked, "What is the solution to the Asian problem?"

It was then that Asians collected themselves, and information from all Asians became the basis for this book.

I was presented with two different groups of Asians that were more than eager to give their two cents. Group A consists of Asians whose approach is to be peaceful and loving, mind their own business, and do nothing to cause confrontation. Their goal is for Asians to do their very best to progress and accelerate in their personal lives. They want to show the world their achievements and accomplishments, believing that actions speak louder than words and everyone will take notice. On the contrary, group B believes that Asians should be more aggressive and let the issues be known to see real change.

I will explain both sides and methods in greater detail:

Group A believes that Asians are being accepted more because they work hard and stay out of trouble. In addition, Asians advance very well academically and progress in their careers; non-Asians see this, and it's a great thing. Asians' automobile and electronics industries currently dominate certain markets, showing the world that Asians can innovate and compete. Furthermore, there are more than enough examples of Asian individuals and businesses accomplishing incredible things from various fields. Therefore, if people stereotype Asians as smart, then that's a great thing, according to group A.

In addition, group A doesn't want people to think of Asians as angry individuals who protest in the streets to get what they want. Asians are constantly overcoming obstacles and achieving miraculous things. Group A argues that it's not necessary for Asians entering a new century to create unwanted friction and tension. This group gave the examples of Martin Luther King Jr. and Gandhi as individuals who improved their people and mankind by nonviolent peace movements.

On the other hand, group B disagrees passionately with group A. They stated that the other group could be dangerous to follow, because their thinking makes Asians weak, complacent, and dependent and seriously jeopardizes the lives of Asians.

Group B stated that Asians could accomplish more and get the respect they deserve if they challenge the wrongs brought upon them. Group B argued that most Asians have always been peace-loving people and minded their own business, and it was Asian haters that intruded and violated Asian affairs disrespectfully, which caused Asians to react and create animosity. Even though Asians achieve incredible things, the very fact that they don't challenge or fight the oppressors is the reason why Asians continue to be victimized, mistreated, killed, and discriminated against.

Group B's best example was Vincent Chin and other numerous stories in which law-abiding Asians were working hard to improve as individuals and as families, minding their own business. Then, without warning, they got hurt or killed just because they were Asian. Group B was trying to demonstrate that Asians must be educated about the world at large and fully understand how people view Asians. This would enable Asians to live in a society where they empower themselves with necessary knowledge to survive, change their ways, move forward, and prosper. In addition, group B considered group A to be like watching fools, and observing an injustice act taking place without doing anything about it. The best example would be that of a home invasion. Instead of getting involved and trying to stop the robbery from continuing, group A would just watch the criminals rob everything they had, in silence and letting them walk off.

Group B concluded that you have to understand the evil of man. When a person, group, people, or race stays ignorant, weak, lazy, unintelligent, or plain stupid, another person, group, people or race will use it to their advantage to oppress those people. Group B wants all Asians to understand history to its fullest extent. They want you to understand the empires of the past and the ruthless leaders, like Genghis Khan, Napoleon, Julius Caesar, and Adolf Hitler. The evil men or oppressors like to commit unspeakable acts on the innocent. Once they have you, they will commit every hideous act and crime against you. Evil people search out other neighbors and murder, rape, pillage, and enslave the ignorant, weak, lazy, unintelligent, and feebleminded individuals. The oppressors ultimately want to commit genocide or have those captured as slaves to do whatever they want with them.

One person I interviewed in Group B, stated that one of the most important things that Asian people should know is, "Once you allow the evil man to assume power, because you decided not to get equal or greater power, then you lose out in the worst conceivable way, when the oppressor decides to use his power and aggression against you." That is why Asians must be immensely educated about the past and do things now to prevent what may happen again in the future. It's extremely important that Asians distinguish who the oppressors are and do not generalize and become them. Once Asians decisively know the three categories of oppressors— those from all walks of life who oppress the Asian people— then they must do their best to defeat and eliminate them. This was the group B's reasoning.

Now that I had opinions from both groups, I decided to combine their viewpoints to write about the solutions to the Asian problem.

XV

THE SOLUTION

While interviewing many of these Asian individuals, I could feel a great deal of anger from them that they'd kept inside for a very long time. It is an anger that will sooner or later blow up combined with the eagerness of change, an anger that will inevitably surface in the future to make a difference.

After I listened and took notes on the interviews I had with various Asian individuals concerning their plight and the injustice toward all Asians around the world, I wrote a chapter dedicated to the solution. Asians should not back down. This is the only solution to the problem, based on hundreds of interviews I had with Asians, and this is what they wanted. Asians should not be derailed or coerced by a non-Asian into thinking otherwise.

If, by any chance, an Asian is sidetracked by a non-Asian to curb his or her thoughts and movement from what is written in this book, then the oppressors planned it that way. This is so that Asians remain weak, and the oppressors can suppress Asians' goals of being successful, independent, and self-empowered. The following steps should be the solution to the Asian problem, and Asians should no longer complain if they follow this ideology.

The solution to Asians' problems can be spelled out clearly—ASIANS:

A: Awareness—Gain a heightened awareness and knowledge of what's going on around you.
S: Synergism—Promote unity, working together as one.
I: Intelligence/Independence—Embrace innovation and self-empowerment.
A: Action—Put thoughts and words into action. Do something. Fight the power!
N: New—A new Asian is created.
S: Success—By following all the steps listed above, Asians will succeed.

———

The following chapters will discuss the steps of ASIANS in greater detail.

XVI

A: AWARENESS

AWARENESS 1:
I encountered a soldier of Asian descent. He said that he served his time in the US Marines for many years but bitched a great deal about not getting promoted and moving up in the military. He blamed it on prejudice from his non-Asian superiors, because he was a vocal Asian. He said he was a very competitive and competent soldier who was overlooked. He observed other non-Asian soldiers being promoted who he felt hadn't proven themselves. He left the military with a sense of betrayal, feeling that he gave so much of his time and effort in the military to be the best soldier he could be. He thought he would serve the military for the rest of his life, until he could retire. Nevertheless, he thought a great deal about Asian problems. He provided me with the "hurt or kill" concept.

It's extremely important that anyone who reads this "hurt or kill" concept does not take it out of context from this book, nor should it be reinterpreted for the purpose of misguiding anyone. If the "hurt or kill" concept is utilized in any inappropriate way—out of context—then it is flawed, falsified, and a straight-out lie.

The Asian American soldier stated that non-Asians will never listen to or take Asians seriously unless they feel the effect of the "hurt or kill" concept. Asians must affect people and society and the world at large. How is this done? What are some examples?

For Asians to be taken seriously and for others to take notice, they must make the oppressors feel that they will be hurt or killed if they don't take notice of the Asian cause. The oppressors must be afraid of you individually, as a group, and as a people and race in order for them to refrain from maliciously hurting or killing you.

For example, if a person is in a room with a small kitten, that individual may not feel that he or she will get hurt or killed. However, if you put that same person in a room with a large, wild tiger inside, that individual may be petrified that he or she will get seriously hurt, devoured, or killed.

Asians are like small kittens who don't fight back, and the world doesn't feel that it will be "hurt or killed" by Asians. That is why non-Asians freely disrespect, denigrate, and discriminate against Asians without feeling a sense of remorse. Therefore, it's important for Asians to transform into ferocious tigers so that the world will take notice and take Asians seriously. From this point forward, if Asians fight and challenge everything that stands in their way, non-Asians will eventually change their thought process about Asian people. Asians must be more confrontational about what they believe in, what's right. Imagine that instead of an Asian in a room being timid, weak, and complacent, that Asian has a sword in hand, ready to chop off your head if provoked. Now that will change the perception.

As a second example, consider a corporation. This corporation enjoys a profitable return on its business, through millions of loyal customers. That corporation wouldn't feel a sense of being "hurt or killed" if there were only one or two unsatisfied customers. However, if millions of the same loyal customers were unsatisfied and no longer did business with them, that company would feel the sense of being hurt financially, or killed, if the business closed down.

Asians should be able to affect the three categories of oppressors financially with their purchasing power. They could affect the world market, businesses, and economies, given Asians' population size. If billions of Asians worldwide decided not to buy what the oppressors were trying to sell, then they could "hurt or kill" a business and surely affect an economy in a massive, explosive way.

People will take Asians much more seriously if they feel their livelihood could be detrimentally affected in a major, direct way through the "hurt or kill" concept. In order for people to change their ways and take you seriously, you have to affect them personally.

AWARENESS 2:

As discussed in earlier chapters, every Asian, whether Asian American or an Asian abroad, must be more cautious when indulging in various forms of media. This includes what they watch, listen to, or read: non-Asian television, movies, newspapers, magazines, music, and radio. They must be very wary. The more they participate in these forms of media without acknowledging the psychological control it has, the more Asians are doomed.

What does this mean? If an Asian were to watch television shows and movies and listen to rock bands without an Asian included in them, that Asian individual is contributing to the propaganda that Asians are not included in society and that Asians have no life but to serve as mental slaves to the three categories of oppressors.

Let's look into it in greater detail. What happens when an individual is bombarded with shows and activities that have no Asians? People from all walks of life, Asian or non-Asian, will believe that Asians are nonexistent and are not important. In the meantime, if you are an Asian who decides to watch and spend your precious time consumed with things that don't include Asians, you are contributing your hard-earned money to people who chose not to accept Asians in their everyday life. Furthermore, Asians are making these people rich and putting them on a pedestal. The oppressors have focus groups that get together, trying to figure out the Asian mind and trying to figure out how they can change and manipulate it for their benefit. Therefore, Asians should combat it and implement their own focus groups to understand other races that the oppressors are from, and how they are operating.

AWARENESS 3:

The oppressors already have it figured out. The beast thinks, "How do you bring an Asian down?" from many different directions and angles. Through many years of domination and monopoly of the minds, the oppressors know not to watch Asian entertainment. They know not to watch Asian sports, buy Asian products or services, or anything else that Asians provide or display. They don't want Asians to be prosperous. On the other hand, the oppressors want Asians to watch them and focus on them and buy into them, because it makes the oppressors marketable and ultimately wealthy and in control. The oppressors truly have it figured out, and "Asian eyes are too slanted to see it."

Mental incarceration is a technique used by the beast. The oppressors are saying to Asians: watch me, hear me, talk about me, buy me, and be my slave, because you have no life but to serve me. Thus, the beast wants to tell Asians that they will only have a life when it says they have a life. It is like injecting Asians with a serum that makes them zombies following the beast.

To illustrate with an example, the oppressors don't watch Asian Ping-Pong and make it a national prime-time event to showcase Asian talent. That's an Asian thing! The three categories of oppressors don't need to focus on it and watch Asian people hit a small plastic ball back and forth on a table. Most non-Asians don't play that sport and ignore it. It's a waste of time and money for non-Asians.

Asians should start thinking the same way when watching sports that don't include Asians, such as American football and other sports. Why should they watch non-Asian people throw a ball back and forth on a field or in a gym when Asians are not benefiting from it? If Asians love watching those non-Asian sports, then Asians must do whatever they can to break into these sports, so they are included in them. This is happening in American baseball; more Asians are gradually participating. If Asians watch sports, entertainment, or any activity that doesn't include Asians, it is equivalent to pathetically watching a bunch of worms crawling and playing in mud. Asians should not waste their time and money on something that's not important or relevant to them.

AWARENESS 4:

Asians who disagree with the solution should ask themselves what they would have done if they were the victims of the stories from the earlier chapters. Would they change their ways and actions, as well as their thought processes? Or would they try to rationalize what happened, only to have those same stories happen to them or their families again in the future? After all, those Asian victims in the past didn't even have a chance to think or rationalize; they just became victims. If those unfortunate, victimized, dead Asians were to be resurrected, and knew what would happen to them beforehand, they would most likely change their ways, if they wanted to keep their lives. For the most part, some of the victimized Asians that was previously discussed earlier in this book, didn't know that they would wake up one morning knowing someone was going to hurt or kill them for being Asian. In a later chapter, I will discuss how an Asian should think moving forward and how to prepare for injustices against them, so that hopefully they could prevent the unlawful acts from happening again. For those Asians that don't think about their protection or sovereignty, they may find themselves taken over, because they didn't take the advice.

AWARENESS 5:

Asian government leaders in some Asian countries have to realize that enslaving their own people will cause a revolt and a backlash. It is detrimental to the Asian cause and unity. If Asian leaders rule as ruthless tyrants among their own people, it creates division and chaos. Conversely, some other non-Asian countries unite with their people and decide it's more productive and profitable to enslave other people of color, like Asians, for their benefit.

Rising Asian countries that are rapidly progressing in power should be cautious in stepping over their boundaries with their neighboring Asian countries. All Asian countries should encourage each other to be more productive and progressive, helping one another to advance in the world market. No Asian country should follow the example of Imperial Japan during World War II, when they disrespected and wreaked havoc upon their Asian neighbors. That experience proved to be fatal, as the animosity against Japan carried on for many years after. Asians must do their best to work with each other, not against each other.

AWARENESS 6:

Asians must understand there will be a time when the Asian haters will make up faulty intelligence and say they need to make a preemptive strike on a particular Asian country and its people, as they did with Iraq. They will make their move decisively and wrongly against an Asian country and its people, knowing quite well their decision is erroneous. So the question is, are Asians prepared for that strike? The oppressors will always make Asians the bad guys, with propaganda through mass media and marketing.

AWARENESS 7:

Asians should always be aware and cautious of how they are viewed, because image is everything. If people view Asians by what they see in the media, in which non-Asians create what Asians should be, then they are susceptible to viewing Asians unjustly. Asian Americans and Asians abroad have to be well aware that what they see on television and in films is not necessarily a reflection of Asians. In addition, most mainstream moviemakers are not Asians themselves. Asians must be well aware that there is hidden propaganda against them to humiliate them and make them look like fools. Moreover, as stated many times before, non-Asian filmmakers make Asians seem inhuman, like cartoon characters. In fact, non-Asian filmmakers try to get the dumbest, weirdest, wimpiest, ugliest Asian actors to play in films, to achieve their objectives of making Asians look like buffoons.

AWARENESS 8:
Being nice, or acting weak, frail, and fragile doesn't work. In fact, it will never work. Only the strong are respected; the weak are laughed at. All Asians must change their ways and not think about being weak. Being passive doesn't work. Asians have been using that tactic for years to be accepted, but apparently it doesn't work. Asians need to change their attitudes and their ways of doing things. Weakness equals disrespect. Stupidity equals disrespect. Ignorance equals disrespect. Not doing anything about the issues equals disrespect. Peace movements, like those led by Gandhi or Martin Luther King Jr. have been done already by all modest Asians. Most would agree, overall, that Asians are already peace-loving people. However, the peace loving attitude didn't work for Asians. It may be time to implement a different approach if Asians continue to be disrespected. The alternative of fighting back if provoked

must be taken; it may be the only solution. Centuries of peace by most Asians were ineffective; most non-Asians laughed at the peaceful Asians, and actually took advantage of them.

AWARENESS 9:
When non-Asians write or speak about anything concerning Asians, Asians should always, with the most meticulous scrutiny, observe what they are trying to say. This ensures that Asians are not fooled into believing a lie. This is because many non-Asians are great experts in manipulating words or text to derail the truth.

When Asians read, see, or hear derogatory things about Asians, through people or any form of media, it should make them extremely angry. This anger should galvanize them to do something about it. Asians will do everything in their power to fight back. Anger as stated before, will motivate Asians to be stronger, smarter, more powerful, and gain the ultimate respect.

AWARENESS 10:
In past times, non-Asians went to various Asian countries and observed the Asian people. They tried to win the Asians' trust, but they planned to divide and conquer the Asians afterward. This is why all Asians should learn history and take it to heart. Once educated, they will never let their guards down, because if they do, they will be conquered when they least expect it.

This is imperialism. History doesn't lie: Hong Kong was taken by the British, Malaysia and Indonesia by the Dutch, Vietnam by the French, the Philippines by the Spanish, and Hawaii by the Americans. When outside countries come to invade an Asian country, they break the nucleus within and destabilize the country and its people, so that it's easier to conquer it and confiscate its goods. This also affects the minds of the Asian people and creates disunity among them, which in turn affects the economy of the land negatively. Thus, sometimes it's difficult for the country's people to get back on their feet again.

The unjustifiable plan of the oppressors is simple. As stated earlier, first win the trust of Asians. Then, when the time is right, conquer and steal absolutely everything from the helpless, oppressed Asians, including their minds and the ways they think. Once in full control and power, the oppressors will preach righteousness and use God's name in the mix to hide the truth, trying to convince the victimized Asians that they should not try to retrieve the power and possession they once rightfully had.

AWARENESS #11
Asians must realize the few good non-Asians don't rule and can't really help the Asian cause. The Asian haters are in office, making the decisions. The exceptional, good non-Asians are only a very small slice of the majority, such as former Governor Ralph Carr from Colorado.

It is imperative that Asians push the issues to the limit, so that all people will know the issues, and eventually, hopefully, the few who respect Asians will become the majority. Only by disseminating knowledge to the majority of Asians can you get to that point.

AWARENESS 12:
Asians don't have to be extraordinarily vocal about the prejudices that happen to them, because Asians are not the type of people who grab picket signs and protest in the streets. There are a few exceptions, such as after the famous killing of Vincent Chin, when Asians united as one. Asians need to know for themselves what's happening around them and keep it in their minds. It's also understandable that causing friction in public could cost them their livelihoods, such as jobs and businesses, so Asians have to play the game right. Therefore, Asians have to achieve their cause in careful, subtle ways.

AWARENESS 13:
Asians must analyze and pinpoint what went wrong. Why did Asians lose their competitive advantage? Why are Asians looked down on? Once Asians identify the problem, then they must confront it and conquer it. Asians must decipher why they got conquered in the past. For example, China was fooled by outsiders, got too involved with opium, and let those outsiders conquer them. Why did Asians, an intelligent race, allow other people to control and dominate them? What happened to the Genghis Khan generation,

when an Asian ruler conquered most of the world? What happened to the Asian dynasties in China? We need to bring them back.

AWARENESS 14:

Before an Asian from an Asian country travels to a non-Asian country, the traveler should be equipped with knowledge, because all Asians should be educated regarding how people stereotype them. All those from various Asian countries who travel to non-Asian countries should take a course to learn how non-Asians view Asians, so that they are not endangering themselves with their lack of knowledge. They could also learn from more experienced, knowledgeable Asians. Asians coming to the United States or another non-Asian country should know what to expect as an Asian individual entering a non-Asian culture. Asians abroad should understand the Asian Americans' wisdom about America and vice versa.

AWARENESS 15:

Asians also have to understand themselves, their various cultures, and how they differ. Asians must be aware of how other non-Asians view their culture and ridicule it. There must be a standard for how Asians will know what is ridiculed and what is not in the mainstream society of non-Asians. Collectively, Asians have to understand what is made fun of and what's not. For example, Asians should know that eating octopus in front of certain non-Asians might not be acceptable in other cultures. It doesn't necessarily mean Asians should change their ways; they should just know how other non-Asians view them in certain situations and circumstances.

AWARENESS 16:

Asians should use Google, YouTube, Twitter, and other well-known websites and search for phrases such as "Asian derogatory pictures," "Asian stereotypes," "Asian racism," "Asian discrimination," and so on, so they can educate themselves about the issues and concerns of Asians. Everyone must know about Asian issues, including the oppressors, so that the oppressors can change their ways and live in good conscience.

AWARENESS 17:

The worst fear of oppressors is that Asians will gain knowledge of what's really going on with the world regarding prejudice and suppression.

AWARENESS 18:

Asian people may have the will and spirit to win, but without money, knowledge, resources, technology, and people to back them up, Asians can't enter any competition in any arena and expect to be victorious. Therefore, Asians must reassess their strengths, weaknesses, opportunities, and threats (SWOT) and get to work.

AWARENESS 19:

The oppressors' supreme goal is to minimize or obliterate the Asian market share in everything. They don't want the Asian markets in various industries to prosper. The oppressors don't want Asian entertainment to invade the non-Asian entertainment world and create any competition. They don't want Asians to sell any products to the world that could create any competition. Oppressors don't want Asians to provide any services to the world that might create any form of competition. They don't want Asians to innovate in technology, medicine, science, and so forth to advance in the world and compete. The oppressors want to monopolize everything and have Asians dependent on them. The oppressors want the master/slave relationship; they want Asians to work for them for free or cheaply. All Asians must do everything they can to avoid this.

AWARENESS 20:

It needs to be reconfirmed that the techniques of polarization and prejudice may be vast and plentiful, and if Asians don't use the same tactics, they will lose everything. Asians must fully understand how the game of polarization is played and take actions to do the same. The beast uses polarization and prejudice to create advantages for the oppressors and disadvantages for Asians.

Polarization and prejudice by the oppressors make Asian haters rich and give them an upper hand. Polarization and prejudice can also create a perception advantage, because image is everything. If Asians are given a bad image orchestrated by the oppressors, then the world's perception of Asians could be harmful and detrimental. Therefore, if the beast or the oppressors use polarization and prejudice against Asians, the Asians should do the same to the oppressors to even the playing field. Asians must be cautious in what they see, hear, and participate in, so as not to make the oppressors wealthy, which, in turn, would enslave Asians.

Asians, for the most part, ignore prejudice but don't realize the catastrophic impact of it. Prejudice against Asians works in the favor of the beast, because oppressors utilize it, but Asians don't.

HOW DOES IT WORK?

As written in previous chapters, the oppressors portray Asians negatively, showing them as wimpy, evil, unromantic, stupid, and nerdy. The effect is that people from all nationalities start to believe it. Thereafter, the win goes to the oppressors, and the loss goes to the Asians. Sadly, Asians don't do anything about the bad portrayal they receive from various mediums such as articles, television, and movies. Again, the win goes to the oppressors and the loss goes to the Asians.

To further illustrate the technique of polarization and prejudice, here are more examples:

1. The oppressors direct the fashion world not to buy Asian clothes or make them fashionable, by not showcasing Asian products internationally. A win for the oppressors and a loss for the Asians.
2. The oppressors make movies that do not show Asians as real individuals, and brainwashed Asians still go to

the movie theaters and pay money to watch movies that do not include Asians. The win goes to the oppressors, and the losers are Asians.

3. A non-Asian male oppressor goes out with a beautiful Asian woman and Asians are OK with it—they don't put up a fight. However, when an Asian male goes out with a beautiful white woman, white people stare and frown at the couple. They are against the relationship and make it known, wanting to create war. There are times when a white male marries an Asian woman and feels he can give his viewpoint about Asian people, because he married an Asian. The white male feels that he can give his opinion, and Asian people shouldn't think he's prejudiced, because he's married to an Asian woman. The white male assumes that his Asian female partner represents the entire Asian race. In addition, he represents all non-Asian males, believing that he's not prejudiced, because he's married to an Asian woman. This is the biggest flaw of them all. Do you think that there might be people of color of various ethnicities and races that love white women but couldn't care less for white males or the white race? Of course. The non-Asian males who marry Asian women should leave their opinions to themselves. The winners are the oppressors; the losers are the Asians for not addressing the double standard.

4. Oppressors exploit, through various mediums, how strange and weird Asians are. The exploitation causes non-Asians to perceive Asians as strange and weird, thus encouraging non-Asians to tease and poke fun at Asians. The result is that Asians are looked at as

cartoon characters instead of human beings and are not taken seriously. The win goes to the oppressors, and the loss goes to the Asians.

5. The oppressors do their very best not to allow Asians to climb the ladder of success in well-known, established non-Asian corporations, by denying Asians high positions. The results are that competent, intelligent Asians are held back from being recruited in top non-Asian companies and are prevented from having positions of power in non-Asian companies. The winners are the oppressors, and the losers are Asians.

6. The oppressors purposely overlook the physical talents of Asians in certain sports. Thus, Asians are not included in certain sports. The result is that Asians are not excelling and showcasing their true talent in those sports, because they are barred from them. The win goes to the oppressors, and the loss goes to the Asians.

7. The oppressors use numerous mediums carefully and deceitfully to portray various Asian products and services as inferior, such as medicine, and then they do not give these items FDA approval. This prevents Asian medicine and other products and services from entering global markets and getting the brand recognition they need to compete with other well-known non-Asian companies. The oppressors win, and the Asians lose.

8. The oppressors, through media, craftily show the world that certain Asian countries enslave their own people, resulting in non-Asian people viewing all

Asians as evil individuals who cannot be trusted. The win goes to the oppressors, the loss to Asians.

9. Asian people look up to and respect some racist white people. Some racist white people look down at Asians. The win goes to the oppressors, the loss to Asians.

There are unlimited examples of how prejudice and polarization are being used by the oppressors for their competitive advantage. The main objective in using this prejudice-and-polarization technique is to dominate and monopolize the market and to obtain extreme power and control over Asian people worldwide and to acquire wealth beyond the oppressors' wildest imagination at the expense of Asians. The prejudice-and-polarization technique is a warlike technique used by the oppressors to win a battle against naïve Asians.

It is imperative that all Asians are aware of how the game is played by the beast, so that they can acknowledge it and play the game better to overcome it.

AWARENESS 21:

When it comes to being stereotyped...*Asians have got it all wrong*!

Most Asians hate it when non-Asians stereotype Asians. For example, non-Asians stereotype by saying Asians are all martial-arts fighters. Some Asians get offended by this, and it dictates their habits and thought processes. Some Asians despise the idea of being stereotyped as martial artists. Those same Asians then disregard and abhor their culture and don't learn martial arts. Afterward, a non-Asian individual might learn martial arts and beat the hell out of those same Asians who abandoned their culture of self-defense. Non-Asian oppressors use psychological techniques to convince Asians to lose their culture of protecting themselves and to let go of something that is a treasure to Asian self-preservation. Asians shouldn't let stereotypes from non-Asians change their behavior and habits.

For those Asians who hate being stereotyped, because supposedly being stereotyped is a bad thing—what if non-Asian people suddenly stereotyped Asians by saying they are all very good-looking, macho, super intelligent, high class, wealthy, and elegant, with fantastic personalities? Would those same Asians who hate being stereotyped be offended and despise the idea of people thinking of all Asians in that positive stereotypical way? The answer is *of course not!*

In addition, would those same Asians suddenly make themselves ugly, lose their muscles and machismo, become stupid, become poor, and have the personality of a jerk so that people do not stereotype them in that positive way? The answer, again, is of course not!

Asians should think extremely hard about the concept of the word stereotype.

The point is that if Asians want non-Asians to stop believing and promoting certain stereotypes, the answer to that problem is unequivocally simple: Asians have to change their ways. They have to dominate and break into other industries, such as mainstream music, entertainment, and other fields that Asians are not known for. The exposure of Asians in these various fields would break those stereotypes. For example, Psy, from Korea, was a major success in the music world with the song "Gangnam Style." He is an example of an Asian breaking into the music world globally.

If many more Asians break into the music world the way Psy did, and fill the airwaves, then the stereotype that Asians are not musical entertainers with worldwide attention would be abolished. This is more incentive to break through, dominate various industries, and get more exposure, so Asians break the stereotypes that they can only do certain things.

> To further illustrate, try to imagine the following:
> Having more Asians in the NBA
> Having more Asians in the NHL
> Having more Asians in the NFL
> Having more Asians in the PGA
> Having more Asians in body building.
> Having more Asians in television and movies as regular actors
> Having more Asians in car racing
> Having more Asians in American politics
> Having more Asians in mainstream music
> Having more Asians in bull riding

Just imagine having more Asians in all other fields, professions, and industries that Asians are not known for. Asians need major exposure in these various markets and to dominate and saturate them for the world to take notice.

Once Asians saturate these various markets, then people will not stereotype Asians as belonging in only one particular industry or profession; Asians should now be motivated to seek other fields that are wide open to them. Endless opportunities will exist for Asians worldwide, if they don't pursue the stereotypical professions that society has chosen and directed them into for benefit of the oppressors.

AWARENESS 22:

If Asians decide not to do anything about the issues and concerns of Asians, then Asian will be buried alive. They will be invisible. It will be all over for Asians. It will be the ultimate doomsday for Asians globally. To further elaborate, the horrific stories previously presented about Asians will continue. Asians will be walking fools, the way they were when writers joked about the Chinese president Hu Jintao with former president George W. Bush with the headline "Wok this Way." They will make fun of Asians such as William Hung, as well as the numerous nerdy Asian characters primarily shown in the media.

People will not take Asians seriously, as evidenced by the previous story from usariseup.com on May 6, 2009 about a young Asian American male who grew up in America but still is treated like a foreigner. Asians will be barred from numerous activities, organizations, and other societies, similar to the way Kevin Kim was treated as an outsider while running for the Nineteenth District City Council in Queens. The stereotypes will not end, and the bad perception of Asians will continue as it did in the magazine *Details*, which showed an Asian man with the caption "Gay or Asian." Asians will be viewed as easy victims who can be killed for fun, like the previous stories of Vincent Chin, an engineer; Minghui Yu, a Columbia University student; Annie Le, a Yale student; Yu Yao, an aspiring lawyer; and numerous Chinese-food deliverymen. Asians will be disrespected with racial slurs like the ones Assemblywoman Grace Meng experienced.

It is because Asians did nothing to change these perceptions that they became easy prey and made non-Asians feel that they could disrespect Asians as they please and step all over them. It's extremely important that Asians realize that if they don't do anything about the issue, their lives could be cut short. He or she could be an aspiring doctor, lawyer, engineer, or productive human being in society with a bright future. But Asian haters want to stalk and kill Asians because they don't consider them real human beings. People will always have negative, incorrect ideas about them if Asians don't do anything about the issues and concerns.

XVII

S: Synergism

Synergism 1:

Every living Asian must change his or her way. All Asians have to be on the same page—one thought, one mind, one movement, and in synergy with the Asian cause. Asians should constantly think of innovative ways to communicate and to unite. Asians must do their best to unify with a purpose. It has nothing to do with having the same political or religious views, but it has everything to do with having the same view concerning how non-Asians think about Asian people in general. The Asian mind-set will permanently change and never go back. The tiny kitten will transform into a ferocious tiger if provoked.

Asian Americans must convince Asians abroad to join the intellectual protest in order to unify a larger audience and influence change. The change for the future depends on the Asian vote globally. Asians will synergize and vote not to buy what the oppressors sell. Asians will vote to boycott the oppressors' interests. It's time for Asians to use their power, their mass population, their money, and their influence.

In America and most of the world, an elected individual is voted in by the majority. The person who is voted into office has the obligation to meet the needs of the majority, because the majority supports that person who is elected. Therefore, it's important for all Asians to stick together, so that they are taken seriously as the majority of the world's population. Thereafter, Asians can create a movement that could change the world.

SYNERGISM 2:

Asians need to gather their resources to aim at the single goal of respect.

There will be power in numbers; people's voices, as well as their intelligence and money, will come into play. Asians, as a whole, have it all. However, Asians need to figure out in solidarity in the way they should be treated by non-Asians. Asians globally have to congregate in their thought process and understand each other, as far as what they feel is offensive and what is not. Asians in various countries differ in opinion when it comes to determine the definition of disrespect for Asians. Once Asians resolve that complex issue of what is considered disrespectful and offensive in the Asian community, then they could move on. As stated before, it will not be about having the same political or religious beliefs but a consensus of how Asians should be viewed, whether in their own countries or abroad; essentially, it's all about respect.

SYNERGISM 3:

What do you do to change or have influence? Well, whether you're an Asian American or an Asian abroad, everyone has to be on the same page. Asians are not all on the same page, and that's what's killing Asians as a whole and as a race. Asians around the globe are the majority of the world's population, and when you look at it from that perspective, Asians are a group that could have major, astronomical influence world-wide. If globalization is the main objective of a changing world that needs to work together and prosper, then Asians must be included in it. However, what steps do Asians have to take to create change? It's a very easy question to answer: unify.

SYNERGISM 4:

Asians should create their own history of the suffering they've endured from non-Asians since the beginning of time, just like the Jewish people, so that Asians can remind themselves constantly that it will never happen again. It would unify the Asian people and make them stronger, smarter, and more knowledgeable. Asian persecution by the oppressors, like the Jewish Holocaust, has to be taught each year to Asians to educate them about the past, so they never forget. Jewish people teach about the Holocaust, so that their people will better themselves and obtain power, and they will not be in the weak position they were in during World War II. It worked, and the Jewish people prospered, improving their livelihoods by uniting as one and placing higher education as their priority. They continue to dominate fields in politics, law, medicine, real estate, business, and everything else that has influence and control. Asians must do the same and learn about the abuse and mistreatment that they experienced and suffered in the past.

SYNERGISM 5:

Asians need a support group, similar to other races' support groups. Asians need their fellow Asians to back them up morally, as well as financially, if needed. Asians have to come out together, in sync, to have their voices heard, from their points of view. Therefore, the consolidation of Asians is imperative. Discipline and focus are key for Asians' ultimate goal of respect. Anger from learning of all the injustice placed upon Asians in the past will galvanize the cause and revolution. An Asian should never feel that he or she is all alone. An Asian should feel that billions of Asians have his or her back and support. If injustice or persecution is wrongfully committed upon one Asian, all Asians should respond to help that Asian.

SYNERGISM 6:

Asians are extremely disciplined and have the tools to facilitate advancement. Asians must treat their Asian counterparts as friends, not foes. Asians should leave the animosity that they have had between them in the past. They should not allow Asian haters to pit Asians against each other, only to divide and conquer. They should move forward, working together.

Asians rebuilding among their countries is vital for progressive change. Therefore, creating harmonious wholeness is imperative.

SYNERGISM 7:

If Asians had a language that was universal among them, then the progress of moving forward could be faster. Therefore, in the future, Asian schools should educate Asian children to speak at least five languages of various Asian countries to build communication among their Asian counterparts.

SYNERGISM 8:

The most important thing that Asians must know about the oppressors is that they don't care about Asians or their objectives. Once every single living Asian knows this and fully accepts that idea wholeheartedly, then Asians can move forward, improve, and prosper, rather than find fake acceptance by the oppressors. Unity in knowledge is vital for all Asians.

The mind-set of all Asians must be uniform and united. Synergism is one of the solutions.

XVIII

I: Intelligence and Independence

In order for Asians to improve and make change, they must fully embrace intelligence and independence. They must use all their resources to empower themselves and become the smartest, most educated, most independent people on the planet. Asians must know everything. The intelligent, independent Asian is an individual that finally understands the Asian issue fully. This Asian is a wounded soldier, or warrior who faced all the discrimination, prejudice, disrespect, bias, double standards, and everything that goes along with being oppressed like a slave. He did not succumb to it and fought to the end, never obeying the oppressors, which would be wrong. The intelligent, independent Asian survives and lives to tell the tale of his or her horrific experience and is now ready to disclose the truth, before the entire Asian population becomes a victim to a world where it has no mind.

What's happening to the Asian people thus far is similar to the original classic film *Invasion of the Body Snatchers*. In the movie, emotionless alien duplicates replace the human population. Asians who are Twinkies and coconuts are suffering from paranoid delusions and are imposters. Nonetheless, it's up to the surviving intelligent, independent Asian soldiers and warriors to go back to their towns, countries, and people to warn them about this horrific phenomenon, informing everyone about Asian issues.

INTELLIGENCE AND INDEPENDENCE 1:

All Asians must strive to be the best in their fields and professions. Asians must be motivated to be the most independent and intelligent people on the face of the earth. This means Asians should not depend on non-Asians to make them successful. Asians must aim to be the best innovators, scientists, doctors, lawyers, engineers, architects, businesspeople, athletes, and so forth. Asians should create a world where they are not dependent on the oppressors, who would fool Asians for their purposes. Asians should utilize their minds to the fullest to be considered the "intelligent Asians." The intelligent, independent Asians are the cream of the crop and the best of the best; they absolutely understand the world around them, and they deserve everything.

INTELLIGENCE AND INDEPENDENCE 2:

For Asians to be intelligent and independent, they must understand that the weak will always self-destruct. In this era, Asians are always looked at as the bad guys, and the oppressors are looked at as the good guys, even though the oppressors are the ones doing bad things. It's all a matter of manipulating the facts, and intelligent Asians should be able to see through the manipulation. Asians must know what the oppressors are thinking about them. Intelligent Asians will observe everything oppressors say, do, and write, as well as what information they disseminate about Asians.

INTELLIGENCE AND INDEPENDENCE 3:
Intelligent Asians know that some non-Asians, Twinkies, and coconuts think differently from Asians. Oppressors think stealing from Asians or doing something similar to that is acceptable and fun. It's imperative that Asians who become intelligent Asians make those ignorant oppressors realize that their reasoning is false and incorrect, and there will be a price to pay if it continues. Intelligent Asians have to stop injustice in its tracks. Intelligent Asians will use the "hurt or kill" concept.

INTELLIGENCE AND INDEPENDENCE 4:
Asians who become intelligent Asians could learn a great deal from the plight of African Americans and other people of color. African Americans are very perceptive about their history and how they are viewed in society in the grand scheme of things. Moreover, African Americans understand what to do to remedy it. They break new ground in society, displaying their talent and intelligence through

sports, entertainment, and education. Asians must also do the same and break new ground. Intelligent Asians will let others know that if they ignore Asians as a people, the others will also be ignored.

INTELLIGENCE AND INDEPENDENCE 5:

Intelligent, independent Asians in America, as stated before, don't want to be white Americans but instead want to be Asian Americans. Similarly, African Americans make their own definition of what being an American means for them. African Americans don't listen to white country music; they make their own music and listen to R and B, rap, gospel, and so forth. African Americans don't follow white America; they define America for their own people. Intelligent Asian Americans must do the same and make their own definition.

Intelligent, independent Asians will have the best of both worlds. This means they will know what their native cultures like and what the rest of the world likes. To further illustrate, a young Asian musician or singer could play and sing music that his or her native Asian people enjoy but could also play and sing music that is liked internationally, by incorporating sounds that are global. Asians must be well versed in everything, such as making fashionable clothes that both their native countries and the rest of the world like. The same goes for food, dance, entertainment, sports, art, and everything else. By doing this, Asians could keep their native culture and transcend to other cultures.

INTELLIGENCE AND INDEPENDENCE 6:

Intelligent and independent Asians will fund research and development more aggressively, so they can market their own products and services for Asians and the world. Asians will develop medicines to compete with brand names such as Tylenol, Bayer, Advil, and other competing companies, such as Pfizer, Johnson & Johnson, and so forth. Asians will have their own competitive social networking platforms to compete with Facebook, Twitter, Google, and so forth. In addition, they will make a soft drink that will compete with Coca-Cola and make a clothing line to compete with Giorgio Armani, Ralph Lauren, Christian Dior, and so forth.

Asians need to develop their own brand recognition. Asians who become intelligent Asians will be more innovative than they have ever been before. Asians will also compete in these markets. Asians must also have their own international press, written from their points of view, so those reading will think independently based on other viewpoints. Asians need their press to be international, so that everyone can read its stories. Competition is feared the most by the oppressors, because it affects their livelihood and standards of living if they can't get you to buy their products and services. Therefore, Asians becoming independent and creating competition would be the things to stop the beast from enslaving them. Doing this instead of relying on the Asian haters or their services would make Asians independent and intelligent.

INTELLIGENCE AND INDEPENDENCE 7:
Intelligent, independent Asians know how the game is played in judicial America and the world. In addition, intelligent Asians will make the playing field equal with their knowledge.

Correction leads to justification; times have changed, and a revolution could change the way the world works when the majority of Asians finally decide to flex their muscles and use their intelligence and independence.

INTELLIGENCE AND INDEPENDENCE 8:
Intelligent, independent Asians know that slavery is not only physical but also mental. Intelligent Asians understand mental slavery is worse than physical slavery, because physical slavery can be seen and felt. Mental slavery is invisible, and it could fool you, stealing your mind, spirit, and soul.

INTELLIGENCE AND INDEPENDENCE 9:
Intelligent, independent Asians have to be the innovators of the world, because innovation is the catalyst to success. Asians must do their best to compete with the rest of the world in all facets of industry. How innovative Asians are is immensely important for advancing to the next level and beyond. Innovation in technology is extremely vital. Advancement in technology is pivotal in order to soar to new heights and improve the modernization of the world's Asian people. Moreover, the quality of the products and services that Asians create and provide must be supreme.

XIX

A: ACTION

Asians must put words to action!

It was Martin Luther King Jr., a pastor, Nobel laureate, and African American civil-rights activist, who stated, "Become a dedicated fighter for civil rights. Make it a central part of your life. It will make you a better doctor, a better lawyer, a better teacher. It will enrich your spirit as nothing else possibly can. It will give you that rare sense of nobility that can only spring from love and selflessly helping your fellow man. Make a career of humanity. Commit yourself to the noble struggle for human rights. You will make a greater person of yourself, a greater nation of your country, and a finer world to live in."

ACTION 1:

Asians have the smarts, discipline, money, and so forth, but their downfall is disregarding prejudice against them as a factor that stifles their success and progress. Unfortunately, if

Asians don't also use prejudice against those who are using it against them, then those others will have an advantage over Asians. If some non-Asian haters, Twinkies, and coconuts exclude Asians from their everyday lives, then Asians must exclude them as well. Asians should be furious about what's happening to them, and they should actively do something about it, until they are in the same playing field as everyone else in every aspect of society.

The Asian mind must change. They must forget about their thinking processes of the past. The Asian cultural mind-set of being complacent, being brainwashed, and following the beast must change. Asians now must undergo a very extensive program of detoxification. It is similar to an individual going through a drug-and-alcohol addiction recovery program. Detoxification is a process that systematically weans Asian people from being addicting to non-Asian media, non-Asian products and services, and so forth. The detoxification is designed to treat the intellectual effects on Asians and remove toxins left in the Asian mind. These are a result of countless years of force feeding by the oppressors through the numerous channels of the media. Studying Asian issues and fully understanding what's gone on with Asians globally since the beginning of time can help one detoxify.

ACTION 2:
Whatever the Asian culture of the past may have taught us about being humble and modest toward non-Asians who don't respect them must be abolished. Asians must utilize the "hurt

or kill" concept, as stated before. Asians should not waste their time with entertainment that doesn't include them. This includes non-Asian TV programs or movies, musical groups, or anything else. This is because the more you participate in this media hype that doesn't include real Asians, the more you help non-Asians with your precious time and money. You also help spread the idea that it is OK that Asians are not included or given a voice.

Asians should not buy movie tickets or music when they are not included. In addition, no time should be devoted to entertainment not involving Asians. Always keep in mind that non-Asians absolutely don't watch Asian entertainment. Once Asians have the knowledge to see TV, movies, sports, and everything else in a different way, they will understand the way the oppressors do their business. Asians should save their money and time to progress their personal achievements and break new ground for Asian awareness and progression.

No Asian country should allow movies that do not include real Asians (not Twinkies) to be a box office hit in their homeland. Asians flocking to non-Asian movies would give the wrong message. After all, most movies made by Asian countries that include only full Asian casts are not box office hits in non-Asian countries, with a few exceptions of stereotypical martial art flicks.

How should an Asian think when watching things that don't include Asians? For example, how should an Asian think when watching programs that the world thinks are so important, such as the Oscars and Golden Globe Awards, which don't really have much Asian participation?

Asians should picture the non-Asian actress with the long gown or non-Asian actor with a suit saying things such as, "I want to thank you for this award and for the stupid Asian people whose 'eyes are too slanted to see' that watch me and support people like me, which is only making our people stronger and letting the pathetic Asian race go unnoticed. Ha-ha!"

As a second example, when watching a sporting event that does not include Asians, imagine a non-Asian athlete accepting a trophy and saying, "Thanks to the dumb Asian jerk-offs for watching our sport that doesn't include them, helping us with funding our sport, and making us wealthy from ratings and sponsorship by Asian individuals and Asian companies."

As a third example, picture the Grammys and imagine hearing a singer or artist say, "I accept this Grammy for all the dumb Asians that broadcast this show to the entire Asian population in their countries, help sell our songs by the millions, and yet keep those strange people invisible and brainwashed."

By seeing things in this way, Asians will realize that they are not included in mainstream society and that they waste their valuable time and money watching and listening to entertainment in which they are not included. Asians absolutely must see things in their everyday lives in a different way, hear things in a different way, and observe non-Asians in a different way. Asians must know how non-Asians think about them based on past stereotypical prejudice and bias. Then they will understand how the world works.

Essentially, this movement is to let the world know that if Asians are not included, are polarized, and are not accepted in mainstream society, then Asians will also choose not to accept non-Asians and polarize them as well. The billions of Asians will surely impact the world and be heard by everyone.

Let the rest of the world's people pay close attention to and use their time for worthless gossip and entertainment from non-Asian celebrities, while Asians think about conquering the world. Instead, Asians should do their best to enter mainstream society in a dramatic, shocking fashion, which some Asians are already doing by breaking new ground and becoming athletes, actors, singers, as well as professionals in other nonentertainment industries and fields. If Asians are to be accepted globally, then they have to struggle and persist in this. Asians have to make their own mainstream society catering to them.

ACTION 3:

Asians have to make their own way to break into international mainstream movies, television, and cable shows. A great example would be the legendary Bruce Lee, a martial artist and actor. When Bruce Lee was denied the lead role in the immensely popular show *Kung Fu* in favor of the non-Asian actor David Carradine, he was very disappointed. Nevertheless, with perseverance, Mr. Lee decided to work with another Asian individual, Raymond Chow from Golden Harvest. Working with other Asians, Bruce Lee became one of the biggest superstars of his time. The moral of the story is Asians working together have to "make their own way" and never depend on the oppressors to bring them up in mainstream cinema or the entertainment world or anything else for that matter.

When it comes to movies, television, cable, or any other medium, Asians must support Asian programs, participate in them, and fund them, because non-Asians definitely will not do it and could not care less about Asian entertainment and its progress. Asians need to have a support base for Asian entertainment.

To resolve the situation and bring more Asians into movies and television, Asians must follow certain rules. Asians should watch more Asian movies and television programs that have Asians in them. In the future, Asian directors, producers, moviemakers, writers, and actors should get together to make more movies that also include non-Asians, so that they will attract a more international audience.

How is this done? Asian moviemakers should be the first to make big-budget universal movies where Asians do not necessarily play the main roles but strong, talented Asian actors with superb personalities cast in supporting roles.

By doing this, gradually global viewers will see more Asians with personalities in films. More frequent positive exposure, which is great exposure for Asian actors in universal films, would make the world more accepting of Asians as real people. Asian moviemakers will *not* be prejudiced like the oppressors. Asians will be the first to include all races in their movies, making them more international. The oppressors shut out Asians based on race; Asians will not follow in their footsteps. Asians will include non-Asians from all over the globe in their entertainment, movies, music, and other mediums. Asians will not carry the same prejudice as the oppressors. Asians will collaborate with numerous non-Asian artists who understand the main objective of working together to achieve exposure for all people in the media. This will help Asians to be more mainstream and help those non-Asians who are assisting in the Asian objectives. It will be a win-win situation for all.

As time passes and more Asians appear in films, those same Asian actors that make up the supporting cast could play main character roles in universal films in the future, roles that are not just about martial arts. It will take time and perseverance, but it will eventually happen as the world changes.

In the meantime, Asians should not get caught up in watching films that do not include Asians. However, if an Asian watches a movie that has no Asians in it, it should only be for the following reasons: to observe how to be a better actor, to learn how to be a better moviemaker, to become a better screenwriter, and so forth. The main objective is to let the world know that if you don't include an Asian in your movies, television, cable show, or other mediums, Asians don't want to support it and make you rich.

Asians should also break into music. Asians entered the mainstream music world very late in the game, but it's definitely not over. As mentioned earlier, Psy, an international music entertainer from Korea, became globally famous with his song "Gangnam Style." He is a great example of an Asian artist who focused on making innovative music, and it received international attention. A new generation of Asian music artists should fine-tune their musical skills and craft them to enter the music industry with a bang. Asian singers, pop stars, musicians, instrumentalists, and various other artists have to incorporate music from all over the world to make their own music and create a unique sound to grab international attention.

In addition, Asians should not get caught up in listening to non-Asian music groups that don't include an Asian artist in them, because these non-Asian artists don't care about Asians. They care only about the money they get from ignorant Asians buying their music. Asians cannot advance in this way.

Therefore, the only reasons an Asian should listen to a non-Asian song are the following: to observe how to be a better musician, to become a better singer, and so forth.

The main objective is to tell the music industry that Asians will not buy your music if you ignore Asian artists and keep them from showing their talent to the world.

In conclusion, Asians must obtain their own home base specific to them. They have to create an international medium where Asians all over the world can watch programs that include Asians. As stated previously, this would be very similar to African American BET programs or Spanish programming such as Telemundo and Univision. Asians will also have programs that cater to them. This home base could be a place where Asians could show and nurture their talent, skills, ingenuity, and more to advance into the global mainstream. It would unite Asians and empower them globally as well as keep them informed of what's happening throughout the world. In addition, Asian programs would be different from the prejudiced oppressors' programs. The Asian programs would include and collaborate with non-Asians in the programs, which would make the programs more international and attractive to everyone, not only Asians. In order to gain international attention, Asians must include non-Asian talents who are willing to work and understand the global cause of the right exposure for Asians and everyone else. Thus, Asians must own their own TV programs, cable, radio stations, newspapers, and other mediums to showcase, nurture, and further Asian talent. They must use English as a form of communication, because apparently it's the most dominating language globally. Here's how it could work: An Asian network is developed that is similar to BET, Telemundo, and Univision. It will be broadcast all across the world, mainly in Asia, America, and other countries that have a high population of Asians. All Asian countries would participate in the funding, such as China, Japan, Korea, the Philippines, Malaysia, Indonesia, Vietnam, and others. This medium will showcase Asian talent in music, movies, TV programs, and other entertainment and news. As Asians begin to ignore other non-Asian programs that don't include them, they will have a medium that they feel at home with, which will empower them to advance in mainstream society. Once other non-Asian programs lose most, if not all, of the Asian market share and profit, their creators will feel compelled to reevaluate their prejudiced ways and include Asians in their programs.

ACTION 4:

In sports, Asians must also make their own way. When it comes to sports, Asians must support their athletes. Asians should not get caught up with non-Asian athletes, because they don't care about Asians. Asians should not be captivated with watching sports that don't include Asians in them, because this wastes valuable time. Asians should only watch non-Asian sports for the following reasons: to observe and become a better athlete, player, or coach.

However, a new generation of young Asian athletes who love these sports should do their very best to venture into these non-Asian sports in order to dominate them in the future. Asians have to support these athletes in every way. For example, in America, Asians must seriously create their own leagues in basketball, football, and hockey to eventually compete with non-Asian athletes. Then, slowly but surely, those proven, talented Asian athletes would eventually be recruited to the NBA, NFL, NHL, and other American sports leagues.

ACTION 5:

Asian Americans should educate Asians abroad concerning how the three categories of oppressors think and feel about Asians. Asian Americans live and breathe with non-Asians daily as well as with Twinkies and coconuts; they know best how the oppressors treat Asians.

Moreover, Asians must talk among themselves, whether one-on-one or in group settings. They should talk in institutions, schools, and so forth to understand and figure out how they're being fooled on an everyday basis by the oppressors. The ultimate objective is to inform every living Asian about how the world is operating at Asians' expense.

Therefore, a Chinese American must educate a Chinese individual in China about the three categories of oppressors, a Japanese American must educate Japanese people in Japan about the oppressors, and a Korean American must educate a Korean about the beast, and so on. America is a microcosm that shows how some non-Asians truly feel about Asians globally. Asian governments must mandate Asian studies in their schools focusing on Asian issues. It's imperative for every living Asian to know how the world views Asians in addition to understanding the plight of all Asians from the beginning of time.

As stated previously, if a non-Asian individual treats an Asian American badly in America, you can be sure that same non-Asian person also hates Asians anywhere in the world. Asians must know these types of people, so that they can prepare themselves in everyday life and business for when they do encounter them.

ACTION 6:
Asians all around the globe must understand mainstream society. Asians who have a dilemma with their identity and clash with those from other cultures should understand personal culture and mainstream culture, and incorporate both. Personal culture comes from one's roots. For example, if you're Chinese but grew up in America, you should

accept your roots but also understand the society around you. Accept other cultures around you and cater the situation to your needs as well as theirs. In order to further their objectives successfully globally, Asians must fully understand the idea and concept of what is mainstream. Asians have their own culture, with its own identity. When they eat their popular, cultural, exotic native food, sometimes non-Asians don't like it, because it doesn't appeal to their own taste buds. In addition, Asians may like the movies and music created in their own countries, but other non-Asian cultures don't get it. Furthermore, in entertainment, an Asian comedian may be funny in his or her own homeland or country but not considered humorous by non-Asian countries. Therefore, as stated before, Asians must understand mainstream culture.

What that means is that Asians living in their homelands need to be more involved outside of their homelands and know what most of the world agrees upon as a standard. To dig deeper, Asians must analyze movies and music that are popular globally, so that Asian moviemakers, artists, and musicians can make their own music likeable and get a broader market share for their products and services.

A great example is when a Chinese restaurant in New York serves Chinese food but also makes fried plantains, tacos, and an assortment of Spanish food to better serve a Hispanic neighborhood. Some Chinese people even learn how to speak Spanish. These Chinese business people get the idea of catering to other nationalities and incorporating mainstream elements into the area they're serving.

In the world of entertainment, Asians should know the difference between what their native cultures like and what mainstream society likes. An Asian comedian should know how to cater jokes to his or her own people but have a set of different jokes for non-Asians. This concept should also apply to movies and music. An Asian moviemaker should be able to make a film for his or her own people as well as a movie that is popular around the world. The same goes with fashion and every conceivable industry out there. Knowing what is current in mainstream society, Asians can delve into what the world around them likes and dislikes, giving them a chance to broaden their grasp of global market share. At the same time, this will preserve their own culture. Given this fact, Asians will have the best of both worlds.

Asians who grow up in America or Europe and have an identity crisis should not disown and feel ashamed of their Asian descent. After all, we don't hear many stories of Americans of European descent discounting their native cultures that have immense, impressive histories, which could be said of other people of color who grow up in America. For the most part, they are proud of their various ethnicities and embrace them. So Asians shouldn't be ashamed of their impressive history either.

It was Cesar Chavez, a labor leader and Latino American civil rights activist, who said, "Preservation of one's culture does not require contempt or disrespect for other cultures… We need to help students and parents cherish and preserve the ethnic diversity that nourishes and strengthens this community and this nation."

ACTION 7:

Asians must understand that other people's business may commingle and correlate with their own business.

The reason why Asians are disrespected, abused, discriminated against, and killed is because Asians decided to mind their own business without realizing that other people's business was related to theirs. Thus, Asians minding their own business and allowing outside, unknown factors to take their course had severe, negative consequences.

In the past, when Asian people living in their own Asian countries of origin were "minding their own business," they didn't realize outsiders from non-Asian countries were secretly planning on conquering these Asian countries, stealing their resources, and enslaving the people. The fact that Asian countries were minding their own business and not thinking of protecting their lands from outsiders gave easy access for outsiders to defeat Asian people and take them over.

Asians must get involved. If they do not, it will be like keeping the door open in a bad neighborhood. Your home will be unprotected, and if you get robbed, it's your fault. Prevention is essential. So when Asian people decide to mind their own business, without minding the business of others, and become uninvolved with what's really going on around them, they bring gargantuan negative consequences upon themselves.

During the Vietnam War, ordinary, law-abiding, innocent Vietnamese citizens believed that minding their own business would keep them from harm's way. But instead they witnessed their homes being burned and their families being killed, raped, and abused by foreign soldiers. Non-Asians use the ignorance of Asians as an advantage for their own benefit. If those innocent Vietnamese citizens had been more involved and informed, they probably would have armed themselves and thought of every conceivable way to protect themselves from outside factors, instead of being clueless, dead sitting ducks.

In modern days, when you hear stories of Asians being discriminated upon, beaten up, raped, killed, and so forth, it is because some of those Asians were minding their own business, not realizing the reality of being Asian.

The numerous previous stories mentioned concerning the victimized Asians were minding their own business and did not realize non-Asian people wanted to kill them just for being Asian. A second example would be an Asian restaurant worker who was robbed and killed while minding his own business, not realizing some non-Asians viewed him as an easy victim. A third example would be Asian women, minding their own business and being targeted for rape and robbery, because they are perceived to be easy prey. If these unfortunate Asian individuals were aware and prepared to defend themselves, maybe the outcome would have been different. If those Asians had a legal gun or any protection to defend himself or was aware that something was about to happen that day, maybe that would have prevented his death.

The moral of the story is that sometimes minding your own business is not always a good idea; you must be much more involved in what's going on around you, beyond just minding your own business. If Asians want to survive and move on in this real world, they must all understand everything that's going on around them. The reason is that you may mind your own business, hoping to stay away from trouble; but sometimes trouble looks for you, and you have to prepare for it.

To change this, Asians must start to mind other people's business that affects them and finally know what's going on around them. Asians should not forget their martial-arts culture. In martial arts, the concept is very simple. You fight, and you defend; you punch, and you block. Therefore, Asians must live their everyday lives the same way. When Asians wake up in the morning, they should ask themselves, "Will I have to fight today or defend myself from outside factors?"

Asians have to finally fight back. They should learn how to protect themselves from the oppressors. Asians must create scenarios and role-play in their minds, like war planners, fighters, warriors, and defenders, so that they are better equipped to protect themselves. Creating scenarios in your mind has nothing to do with being paranoid. It has everything to do with safety and your livelihood. It should be second nature and common sense, similar to looking both ways before crossing the street so you won't be hit by a vehicle.

In previous stories, you heard about many innocent Asians being victimized, such as the fast-food Chinese deliverymen; Asian students; Asian drivers; Asian women; innocent, ordinary Asian individuals; and so forth. Thus, Asians should start thinking of what they should do if faced with these same situations. If Asians see someone looking at them in a way that makes them feel they might be harmed, then they should be prepared to fight, defend, and conquer. If Asians hear someone screaming out racial slurs and epithets, then they should be prepared to brawl and win. If Asians happen to have a weapon with them when facing these troublemakers, then they should use it. If Asians do not have a weapon, then they should look for the closest item that they could use as a weapon to defend themselves. After Asians defend themselves from an Asian hater, and the hater is knocked out cold, they should call their lawyers and say that they had to defend themselves and then call the police. Asians should no longer be perceived as easy victims but as ferocious fighters.

Asians must learn how to fight like supreme warriors. They must study the art of war. Asians must learn all the various disciplines such as martial arts, boxing, wrestling, street fighting, military warfare, and every conceivable art of war to protect and defend their livelihoods. Asians must make their own scenarios of how to handle various situations in order to live and survive. For example, if Asians go out and see people wanting to do harm to Asians, then they should know how to handle themselves to avoid being harmed or killed.

ACTION 8:

The Asian American community and Asians abroad have to take things to another level and use the hurt-or-kill concept. They have to boycott businesses that don't support the Asian cause, and they have to make it well known, so those businesses lose profit. Being polite most of the time doesn't work; sometimes the hurt-or-kill concept is a more effective method. Asians have to research, single out, and expose those companies, organizations, and businesses that are prejudiced toward Asians and try to shut them down by boycotting them. The entire Asian race has to figure out how they can cut off the money supply of the oppressors, so that they cannot continue to operate and prosper. Asians must do a better job securing their own money and funneling their funds back to their own community in order to grow and progress. They must make it extremely difficult for the oppressors to capture the Asian market and its wealth.

The purchasing power of Asians worldwide is powerful. There are billions of Asians globally, and the Asian market is vast. Therefore, Asians literally have the power to make a company profitable or bankrupt it, if they want to. Limiting the oppressors' resources and affecting their flow of money is key to halting their power. Asians have to make sure they're not directly or indirectly funding or supporting the oppressors' objectives. It would definitely get the oppressors' attention if Asians affect their money supply. Asians should not buy or participate in what the oppressors are trying to sell. Eventually, the oppressors are going to change their ways and cater to Asian needs and concerns, as they feel their financial bottom line change dramatically.

ACTION 9:
Asians should have a personality that is welcoming but fierce if provoked, similar to a dragon, which is calm if left

undisturbed but ferocious if irritated. Asians should dictate how people look at them, not the other way around. Asians will not be looked at as weak victims but as people to be reckoned with. Asians should display a formidable persona, ready for confrontation.

ACTION 10:

Asians should urgently begin a competition and enter it. Very similar to the space race (or the nuclear race) between Russia and the United States, Asians must enter a race of intelligence and power. They should enter every conceivable race. Asians must dominate the various fields of the world including science, sports, education, and more. Asians have to enter the world of competition like a culture or religion and lead the way. Asians globally must modernize their standard of living to compete with other industrial countries.

ACTION 11:

There should be a code that Asians live by. Asians should never have a condescending, negative discussion about Asian issues in front of non-Asians, because some non-Asian haters may get involved, causing debate and more friction among Asians. Asians' quarrels and disagreements should be kept behind closed doors. Always keep in mind that non-Asians' objectives are to create disunity between Asians.

Therefore, any Asian should respect another good Asian unequivocally, just for having good Asian character.

ACTION 12:

Asians have to develop a great personality to be likeable and appeasing. Asians should also learn the personalities of other cultures, so that they can contour their own personalities to other cultures' likings. The more that isolated Asians know about other non-Asian customs and cultures, including engaging socialization, the better they will understand people as a whole. Being ignorant about other people's ways of life and concerns will be self-destructive. Being ignorant, period, is deadly. Asians should be able to fit in with any personality and understand people from other countries and cultures.

ACTION 13:

Asians should challenge everything negative that is said about them by the three categories of oppressors. Non-Asian people like to write about Asians, whether it's as an individual, a group of people, a race, or a business corporation, for the purpose of painting a negative picture. It's time for Asians to counterattack and write about those non-Asians in the same way. They need to write things to combat non-Asian writers writing about Asians. They also need more Asian writers writing about non-Asians.

ACTION 14:

Asians must change the way they do business with the oppressors. Asians must understand how they are thought of and perceived by the oppressors, so they are prepared when the oppressors try to fool them.

ACTION 15:

Asians must have a mental protest. Asians won't necessarily change their behavior in front of non-Asians. In fact, they will still associate and hang out with the three categories of oppressors, just like they normally do. But they will just be a little more cautious and aware of what's going on around them.

As time goes on, non-Asian haters will finally get it. They will realize they lost the Asian market share, and their livelihood has changed for the worse, because Asians affected non-Asian businesses and their profits substantially and in secrecy. Underestimating Asians will be the last thing oppressors will do.

Those non-Asians who choose not to understand the Asian issues will perish and die from a hidden cancer, slowly but surely. The cancer of ignorance will eat up the gullible people as they see their wealth disintegrate when billions of Asians no longer buy what they sell, or work for them or with them. Those non-Asians, Twinkies, and coconuts that go through their everyday lives not knowing the true conscience of an Asian, let alone true knowledge about Asians, will experience significant, unforeseeable loss. When they least expect it, suddenly...Bang! It's too late, and everything will go haywire for those who chose to be ignorant about Asian issues, because anyone who chooses not to worry about another person's thoughts and concerns is doomed eventually.

ACTION 16:

Asians should have a much more astronomical mission, similar to African Americans' cause for respect and equality. Asians also endured slavery. Asians will be victorious when united. The mission is to have every single Asian understand the issue, whether they agree with it or not. Similar to how Jews inform their people and others about the Holocaust—through mass media, every chance they get—Asians need to broadcast their own holocaust as well. Asians need to disseminate this information through print, airwaves, music, television, radio, movies, the Internet, and every conceivable medium to get the word out. It will take Asians to tackle the issue through the media. They have to broadcast their issues, utilizing the Internet through well-known websites, such as Google, Yahoo, Facebook, Twitter, and many others to communicate their message. Asians should gather together to inform Asians about the issues, at home or in schools, clubs, political arenas, focus groups, and so forth with the intention of having Asian issues heard by every living Asian in the world.

ACTION 17:

If any non-Asian American asks an Asian American where he or she is from, the Asian American should immediately reply back to that person by asking the same question. If that person says "America," then the Asian American should ask what nationality that person is. The person who asked is trying to imply that the Asian American is not an American. Thus, that person is trying to belittle an Asian.

ACTION 18:

Any mistreatment of an Asian by a non-Asian public official must be investigated, so that racist officials don't take advantage of naïve Asians. Sometimes public officials of non-Asian descent abuse their power against Asians, based on prejudice. Asians must look out for that. Asian lawyers are needed to represent Asians. In fact, more Asian lawyers are needed to protect Asians from injustice in America and worldwide. It's imperative that the best Asian lawyers represent the innocent Asians and bring the issues to the global public forum, so the world sees the injustice.

Thus, any injustice that happens to an innocent Asian should go viral worldwide. All forms of media should be utilized including Facebook, Twitter, and the entire information highway. This is to encourage every living Asian to gather as one to back up an Asian whom an injustice was committed upon.

In addition, all Asians must collectively and fully back up any Asian mistreated by a non-Asian until the end.

ACTION 19:

Asians from various countries and ethnicities must tell the world of their similarities within the Asian global communities, as well as of their differences from their Asian counterparts. And Asians should be respected for that. Asians should learn from other races with similar struggles. African Americans were very successful in their contribution to the movement for equality. Martin Luther King Jr., Malcolm X, and a host of African American activists came forward to demand their acceptance in American society. And so should Asians. Asians are either very silent in their approach or don't have the correct means to grab the national attention like other activists of non-Asian descent, such as African Americans or Hispanics. Asians must also be activists for the rights of Asians and bring out passionate, prominent individuals to represent Asians.

ACTION 20:

Asians have to form a powerful organization to unite, which is essential and pivotal. There are probably some Asian organizations out there that are good, but they need a very aggressive organization with passion to make a real change for Asians all across the world. Once Asians make an absolute, conscious decision en masse, the revolution of the mind will begin. Asians must be actively conscious of changing their mind-sets in order to change the things around them.

ACTION 21:

Asians have to be prepared. Asians have to understand the concept of unpreparedness as well as what it means to be being weak and ignorant. Asians have to research and analyze the history of the world. Asians need to realize that countries that were annexed and conquered in the past were countries that were unprepared. These Asian countries that lost their land, property, resources, and the people's dignity and respect were countries that did not think about their national interests and security. Therefore, these Asians were not ready when the aggressors decided to take everything away from them, including their land. This is why all Asian countries should be prepared rather than unprepared. It means building their militaries, advancing their technological capabilities, and changing the mind-sets of their entire population.

ACTION 22:

Asians must learn to use their skills and do so expeditiously to gain lost ground. Asians' actions must catch up with the world. Most Asians are asleep and not aware of the issues. Once they feel the impact and acknowledge the concerns of Asians, they have to progress and move forward quickly, so they can catch up with the rest of the world and compete in all the various fields that they are lagging in.

ACTION 23:

The members of the Association of Southeast Asian Nations and Japan must get together to make it mandatory for all Asians to know about Asian issues through various institutions. They should create a book of knowledge. They must implement Asian studies and education in schools throughout all of Asia. All the various Asian governments must implement mandatory education in schools for Asians concerning Asian issues.

ACTION 24:

The minds of Asians must be strong and alert. Asians should always be skeptical when dealing with the oppressors; knowledge of history will prove that. It would be unfair to have Asian haters gather their tools to eliminate and exterminate Asians, while Asians are unguarded, ignorant, and not prepared to defend themselves in an inevitable attack.

The three categories of oppressors should not be allowed to silence Asians like a judge in a court. Asians must speak out for the rights of Asians. Now, Asians will have to find a solution. The ultimate solution will be strong, direct, and aggressive, but Asians, at the end, will have results.

ACTION 25:

The only way for the world to respect Asians is for them to obtain as much power as they can. The oppressors of the world do not listen to modesty or weakness; they actually prey on those with that ideology. When former US president Harry Truman left office, he gave his first major speech in Philadelphia and attacked the current president at the time for proposing to cut defense spending. Truman said, "Big talk does not impress the rulers of the Soviet Empire." He then said, "What impresses them are planes and divisions and ships." This is why Asians should be the best they can be.

The three categories of oppressors don't respond well to Asians' big talk on change or their dignified custom of humbleness. Asians have to be out there, dominating, to show the world that they're doing it and what they're made of. Thus, every living Asian should strive to be the best and obtain power and intelligence beyond people's comprehension; that is what will get the oppressors' attention and respect. The world must fear you to respect you; therefore, Asians must live every day doing their best to become as smart and powerful as they can. Asians must plan their schedules accordingly every day as they live their lives. They must learn how to obtain that intelligence and that source of influence and control. This is the only solution to the problem—to add action to their new mind-sets. Asians must push the envelope.

Asians must break into mainstream society and end the unfair portrayal or stereotypes society has about Asians.

Asians must boycott items and use various methods to combat the psychological technique utilized by the oppressors.

ACTION 26:
Asians right now have to experience a civil war just like the American Civil War to end slavery. Asians have to fight the bondage of intellectual slavery. And it's going to be a very tough war, because Asians are fighting very formidable opponents, such as Twinkies, coconuts, and plain idiots. Asians should unite in their thinking, whether they are abroad or domestic. Asians have to get together to conquer the unseen intellectual slavery that traps them. Asians have to change their thought processes, which have been corrupted by the oppressors since the start of time.

ACTION 27:

Asians must become leaders, not followers. To be included in mainstream society, Asians have to be pioneers and in the forefront; if not, then they are followers, carelessly being misled by the oppressors.

ACTION 28:

When Asians no longer spend their time watching and listening to the lives of the oppressors, then Asians could now have a life of their own. A world of opportunity will appear. Asians will be inspired and motivated to seek new careers and embrace new professions and industries that are awaiting them, ones that were not considered before. It's also going to be vitally important for Asians to be the smartest people that they can be, with all this newfound time to improve.

Asians will now value the concept of "opportunity cost." Asians give up opportunity by spending their time and effort in something that doesn't benefit them and is considered unproductive to the Asian cause. Therefore, the time Asians consume watching, listening, and participating in non-Asian activities will now be devoted to things that will benefit Asian productivity.

ACTION 29:

The Asian male has been disrespected through various mediums for far too long. Part of society's goal is to emasculate Asian men so that they can portray them in a bad light.

Asians should take advantage of that knowledge and know what's out there, so that Asians can improve and abolish that stereotype and advance. The disrespect of Asians will cause billions of Asians to rise up and finally fight back. And the new Asians should program themselves to think differently.

Asians all over the world have proven themselves intellectually. However, they neglect to concentrate on other fields in which they do not dominate. Asians should concentrate on and develop their physical attributes and talents. There has to be a balance. Yes, it's OK to be intellectually sound, but one should be physically challenged as well. Things are changing as we see more Asian athletes coming of age, but we need more.

Many Asian women are turned off by Asian males, because the men have neglected their own physical aspects. The stereotype of geeky Asians is also a reason why many Asian women date non-Asian men. Asians must do a better job taking care of their physiques, not only their intellect, to change the perception. Truly a new age and generation must evolve. Asians must face, capture and take possession a new beginning with a calling, a determination, a goal, and a mission to win an invisible war. While most Asian males focus so much in school, cramming for their studies and losing sleep, their physical bodies have deteriorated, making them frail and geeky. Time management is vital to that problem and balance.

The new Asian male must exercise, working out routinely and effectively, and have a healthy diet to aim for supreme physical shape. The determined young Asians who make up the new generation will train their bodies intensely to become elite, unstoppable fighting machines with bodies like Adonis. Asians will join the gym en masse with the determination to build their bodies like no one has ever seen before. The new Asian male must get with the program. The new Asians will get the rest and sleep they need to be trained like ultimate warriors, bringing back their warlike, innate cultures of the past and learning from their mistakes.

ACTION 30:

Asian males must take care of their penes and take immediate action. For whatever reason, people have said that Asians have small penes. This struck many Asians that I spoke with. Some Asians, who wanted to show their penes to prove they weren't small, gave lots of advice. This was a stereotype that evolved because some Asians, who didn't represent all Asians, probably showed their small penes on videotapes for everyone to see. Or some scrawny, naked Asians in a locker room walked around, embarrassing the rest of the Asian population. Nevertheless, in a society of billions of Asians, you would think some people are fat or skinny, some are short or tall, some are good-looking or ugly, and some have big penes or small penes. Yet people, for some reason, decided that all Asians have small penes.

It is similar to Asians that have scrawny, frail, and weak body frames. The physical body will stay skinny and frail if you don't work at it. Thus, many intellectual, bookworm Asians are so engulfed with their studies or schoolwork that they don't take care of their physical bodies and penes. An athlete, whether Asian or non-Asian, will have a much more muscular physique when compared to that of a nerd who doesn't exercise.

My Asian interviewees with big penes gave advice to Asians that may have small penes. They advised these individuals to actively concentrate on their penes. They said a penis is a muscle, not a bone. If you work out your bicep, it gets bigger, and a penis is similar. What you eat and consume also makes your muscle or fatty tissue expand. In addition, the younger you are when you start focusing on your penis, the bigger, longer, and better your penis becomes. When my interviewees had this long, amusing conversation with me, I didn't ask where they were getting the information from or for facts to back it up, because I didn't feel inadequate myself. So I don't know how scientific their information was. Actually, I didn't want to write about this topic, because some readers might find the subject matter inappropriate. Nonetheless, it's important to know the negative views people have about Asians. In a nutshell, their main point was to actively focus and nurture the penis, and pay attention to it. Some Asians who say they have big penes want those Asians who are small to get with the program. Therefore, those Asians who have small penes must urgently do whatever they can to get bigger penes. If they have to read various and numerous books on how to make their penes bigger or change their diets and sleep patterns or get full, maximum erections a hundred times a day to make their dicks as hard and expanded as they can, then they must do it to change the perception. Abrasively, those Asians who gave their point of views, were sick and tired of this stereotype and angrily stated once those Asians who are small get with the program, and get their dicks as big and plump as they want them to be, then they must fuck the world!

ACTION 31:

The new, knowledgeable Asians should live their lives as the aggressors and be intellectual, strong, and determined. Asians must do whatever they can to resolve the issue. Mental polarization of others is essential for Asians to compete. Asians must start creating real competition, aggressively, so the oppressors don't dominate with a monopoly.

ACTION 32:

This is a very sensitive, controversial topic, but it needs to be addressed seriously. Asians should ask themselves if they like being Asian. If it's too much to live life as an Asian, then that person should do him- or herself a favor and make a decision. Live life and be a productive and valuable Asian, who's a fighter, or…simply kill yourself.

If you are an Asian who hates yourself because society forced you to hate yourself, then you are a weak fool. There's no reason for you to live; you're only going to live a life agonizing that you're not something you want to be. In fact, you're going to just spend your life denigrating and hating Asians and finding ways to destroy the Asian species, because you hate yourself so much for being Asian. You'll then be body snatched to become a Twinkie or coconut, which is an Asian hater. Why bother? No need to hurt yourself and others; you're better off dead than alive. This is the viewpoint of many Asian activists who are passionate about Asian issues, and they truly abhor Asians who hate other Asians. They consider those Asians "stinks"—stupid chinks. Asians who hate other Asians are lost souls who don't know what's going on.

Asians never requested to be viewed with pity. Thus, Asians have to start a new generation that is not ashamed. Asians need to weed out the weak and keep the strong.

Asians have to choose how they want to live their lives. There are only two options. Live like a slave, like a fool, and be disrespected; or live free and have the ability to live your life the way you want it to be, with respect and honor. The choice is yours.

In conclusion, once Asians finally decide not to waste their valuable time with non-Asian activities, they will have an enormous amount time for themselves. Therefore, Asians can utilize their time to improve themselves. They will become geniuses. They will work out their physical bodies to become the ultimate elite warriors. Asians will break new ground and create opportunities, no longer depending on non-Asians to create those opportunities. Asians will then get together in billions to become one, for one sole purpose… *respect*. Thus, a new Asian is born.

XX

N: A New Asian is Born

When Asians reach the point where they fully understand how the world works and embrace it, accept it, and do not deny it, then a new breed of Asians will arise. The new Asian will be different and more determined and successful than any previous generation. Once Asians have complete knowledge about Asian issues and absolutely know what's going on, it will be time for a new beginning. Equipped with wisdom, Asians will sleep a very long, restful night. They will awaken to a new morning with a calling, determination, goal, and mission to win an unseen war for change. A new generation will be born—the ultimate, elite Asian, a metamorphosis that people have never seen before…the new Asian.

- The new Asian is unafraid to seek new opportunities from various professions, careers, and industries.
- The new Asian male is stronger and bigger and has more power from the intense physical workout program he creates for physical supremacy.

- The new Asian is better looking from taking care of his or her physical appearance and having better hygiene.
- The new Asian is a superior warrior, learning the various arts of war, such as martial arts, boxing, wrestling, street fighting, and military warfare.
- The new Asian is ready to conquer in war if challenged.
- The new Asian is well-mannered and respectful, educated on international etiquette.
- The new Asian will be more disciplined than ever, trained to overcome any obstacles in the way.
- The new Asian will strive to work as hard as it takes to accomplish any task.
- The new Asian-controlled mind-set will be extremely focused to achieve any goal and objective.
- The new Asian will learn many languages to work and communicate with people all around the world.
- The new Asian is healthier from a regimented diet and lives longer.
- The new Asian is more athletic and competitive and participates in every sport.
- The new Asian is more intelligent, utilizing brain power to the maximum, diligently spending valuable time learning everything.
- The new Asian mentally boycotts everything that doesn't include Asians.
- The new Asian doesn't waste time on things that don't advance the Asian cause.
- The new Asian uses valuable time and money on self-improvement.

- The new Asian doesn't waste time and money for the benefit of the oppressors.
- The new Asian has a better, much-improved personality and social skills from interacting with numerous people of various ethnicities.
- The new Asian is adaptable to any culture or way of life.
- The new Asian will never succumb to becoming a Twinkie or coconut.
- The new Asian knows fully how the oppressors' thought processes work, from experience and learning what happened from the beginning of time concerning the Asian plight.
- The new Asian doctors will strive to be the best doctors in the world providing elite medical service.
- The new Asian engineers will strive to be the best engineers developing amazing unique advancement in the world's infrastructure.
- The new Asian lawyers will strive to be the best lawyers in the world fighting injustice.
- The new Asian chefs will strive to be the best chefs, utilizing the vast ingredients of the world to make the perfect dishes.
- The new Asian athletes will strive to be the most competitive athletes of the world.
- The new Asian scientists will discover cures to cancer and other ailments and further advance science to improve the world.

- The new Asian will be the innovator of the world, making, developing, and designing new products and services for everyone globally.

In a nutshell, the new, focused, profound Asians will astonish and surprise the world with their incredible abilities and ingenuity.

XXI

S: SUCCESS

Asians first have to acquire knowledge and be *aware* of everything that's going on around them and break away from the mental slavery. Second, Asians must use *synergism* and work together with the entire Asian race worldwide. Third, they must educate all other Asians to become *intelligent* and *independent* and learn from each other concerning the issues that affect them. Afterward, Asians have to put decisive *actions* to everything they learned, and make their own way. Once Asians have obtained the necessary knowledge they need to empower themselves from within, they will sleep a very long night and awaken as *new* Asian individuals, certain it was God's will not to allow the oppressors to suppress Asians any longer. Finally, the new Asian generation will have opportunities they never had before. Once Asians follow the steps of awareness, synergism, intelligence/independence, and action and start new, with a clean slate, they will achieve incredible *success* in whatever they do and move forward to an unbelievable new world that awaits them.

If Asians follow the protocol mentioned above, they will be the breakthrough race. Furthermore, if the attitude and psyche of the Asian mind changes worldwide, then it's game over for the Asian haters.

Asians will be galvanized and not fearful of entering new territory in international arenas of various industries and careers they have never entered before. Asians will challenge themselves like they never have before. Asians will have opportunities like they never have before. Asians, in sync, will get respect like they never have before, as the world realizes that, finally, billions of knowledgeable Asians are working together as one to make sure they get the respect they deserve. Thus, once Asians unite for their purpose, change and progress is inevitable.

XXII

Conclusion

Throughout the chapters of the book, you may notice similar repetition in the passages, wordings, and meaning. This was done purposely to reiterate and ingrain the message into the psyche of the Asian mind. The meaning of all this is for Asians to realize that people, without a doubt, are prejudiced against them. Asians absolutely must know, accept, and embrace this. They must start a revolution. In addition, this book was a cry from very passionate, concerned Asians to inform other Asians everywhere that if the issues are overlooked and their concerns are abandoned, then all Asians will be subject to the ultimate slavery by the oppressors. Slowly but surely, Asians everywhere will be transformed and brainwashed to become Twinkies and coconuts. Once Asians morph into Twinkies and coconuts, they will serve the oppressors until death do them part. They will buy whatever the beast has to sell, follow what the beast has ordered them to do, work tirelessly for the beast, be disrespected by the beast, be forced to listen to what the beast has to say, be denigrated by the beast, and eventually be killed by the beast without justice.

These articles have one main theme: some people are unequivocally against Asians. They don't like Asians. Asians have to change their lifestyles to improve, while remaining aware of how some non-Asians, including Twinkies and coconuts, are fooling them. Asians should never compromise their integrity just to be accepted by non-Asians. Asians should not try to find acceptance by artificial people. As Asians embark upon their quest for righteousness, they should do so with careful precision in order not to prejudice others. When Asians form powerful Asian groups, they should not be created to someday fight against each other because of a misunderstanding. They would lose the main objective, Asian unity, and this would implode the Asians' cause.

The point of this book was to make the world aware of Asian issues. Furthermore, it was written to convince all Asians, in a clear manner, that they have been made fools of by the oppressors far too long—from the beginning of time. And if Asians don't educate themselves and change their ways, they will be at the mercy of the beast.

Once the Asian haters, oppressors, or the beast come to realize that all Asians are now educated and knowledgeable about the issues, they will have no choice but to change their ways. The Asian haters cannot prosper, profit, and excel on the world stage without Asians. The Asian market is way too gargantuan to avoid. Thus, change begins when all Asians are on the same page.

As stated before, this book is, without a doubt, the most comprehensive modern book ever written about Asian issues.

As said in the beginning of this book, I was somewhat reluctant and unsure of writing about this topic, because I did not want to be classified or thought of as a writer of political issues. Nevertheless, as stated before, I reminded myself that if I'm a writer, I should be able to write about anything, and my previous diverse stories in various genres prove this.

Hopefully, people reading this book will interpret the message in a positive way, as a catalyst for change and respect for all people. Furthermore, I hope the book will begin a discussion about all people uniting as one to work together in peace and harmony.

THE COVER PAGE
WEAPONS OF ASIA

1. BRUNEI MILITARY SWORD
2. RARE CAMBODIAN DARB DHA SWORD
3. CHINA'S SWORD OF BRAVERY
4. INDONESIA'S TRADITIONAL KRIS-KERIS WEAPON
5. JAPAN'S HONJO MASAMUNE SWORD
6. KOREAN JIKDO SWORD
7. LAOS AVERY FINE SWORD
8. MALAYSIAN KERAMBIT
9. MONGOLIAN KNIFE SWEAT GOLDEN SWORD
10. MYANMAR DHA (SWORD)
11. PHILIPPINE'S KAMPILAN SWORD
12. SINGAPORE SLING WRAPPED FULL TANG MACHETTE
13. THAILAND KRABI-KRABONG
14. VIETNAMESE NINETEENTH-CENTURY DADAO SWORD